To Understand Your Child

"Trust in the Lord with all your heart and lean not on your own understanding."
— Prov. 3:15 NIV

To Understand Your Child

by

KAY KUZMA, Ed.D.

Published by

Box 2222
Redlands, California 92373

First copyright © 1978 by Pacific Press Association under title *Understanding Children.*

Second copyright © 1985 by Parent Scene, Inc.

Revised, 1985

ISBN: 0-910529-00-0

Printed in the United States of America.

I Dedicate This Book

. . . to the children I have taught and who have taught me more about understanding children than have textbooks and degrees.

First, to the many children I have worked with in nursery school, child-care and church programs, from whom I have learned that every child is special in his own way and must be loved for his uniqueness and dealt with individually.

Second, to my own children — Kimberly, Karlene and Kevin — who have helped me understand why parents so frequently told me before I had children, "Wait until you have your own!"

It takes a heap of understanding to love a child into maturity. But I've also discovered that there is no greater satisfaction than combining the joy of teaching other children with the joy of teaching one's own.

...and I Wish To Thank ...

. . . My husband, Jan, for understanding me — while I've been trying to understanding children!

. . . My colleagues who have challenged me into a deeper understanding of children: June Patterson, Ethel Young, Paul Roesel, Wilma Phillips, Toini Shobe, Marilyn Beach, and so many more.

. . . My dedicated staff who have lightened my load and made it possible for this new book to be published: Lynn Ritter, Liz Maryanski, Barbara Wilkins, and Craig Turley.

. . . My friends: May Chung, who believes in opening doors of possibility; Dick and Carol Weismeyer, who have donated their services and time; and Raylene Phillips, who worked with me shoulder to shoulder during the final count-down days.

CONTENTS

Preface

For most parents, understanding children is a work of a lifetime, for each new child or grandchild is uniquely different.

When a child is rightly understood, accepted and molded, the child's God-given personality traits are free to blossom into the mature characteristics of love, joy, peace, longsuffering, kindness, goodness, faithfulness, gentleness, and self-control. (Galatians 5:22-23)

However, if a child feels misunderstood, rejected and manipulated, negative traits can readily develop and too often the result is bitterness, conflict and rebellion. Many times this happens when parents willfully impose their own preconceived opinions of how they should "train up a child in the way he should go."

There is no 100% guarantee in life. Every child must ultimately choose the way he or she will go. But, the chances of influencing a child toward the positive can be significantly increased if parents would just devote a few extra hours when a child is small to learn about typical child development and behavior. With this knowledge, you, as a parent, can more effectively guide your child throughout his growing years and be the first and most important teacher in your child's life.

To Understand Your Child is child psychology made easy and practical. This is a book to help parents gain insights into their child's unique character and developmental behavior. But that's not all; it also gives practical suggestions about how parents can mold their children so that they will grow to be happy, loving and productive individuals.

God bless you in your lifelong task of understanding your child.

Kay Kuzma
Redlands, CA

Though it cost all you have, get understanding. Prov. 4:7 NIV

Understanding Children's Needs

Understanding children's needs and how these needs can be met is the first requirement for parents of young children. This knowledge can come only in part from the Scriptures, textbooks, and the lecture hall. One must also be willing to learn from the child — to pick up clues from his* behavior and words concerning his particular needs at a particular time. Then, by putting all this information together, parents must put their skills and energy into the task of trying to meet each child's needs.

Children Need to Be LOVED

Your child's first and foremost need is simply to be loved. Every child is like an empty cup, and the only way the cup can be filled is by showing the child love. It is only when the cup is filled to overflowing that the child can give love. Your child needs to be cuddled, to be held, to feel close to you, to feel emotionally comfortable and warm, to be wanted and to be understood. Meeting children's physical needs for food and care is not enough. Many children have failed to thrive and have

*Please note that I've used the masculine form of pronouns only for convenience sake. When you read "his" please think of "her," too.

even died, in spite of adequate physical care, because of the absence of love. Love is so important that you, parents, must fill this need before any other. It is not enough for you to *feel* or *think* or even *know* that you love your child. Your child, himself, must *perceive* that love or it is meaningless. Showing your child that he is loved is especially important during the early years.

If you ask parents, "Do you love your children?" they will often say, "Of course. I give them what they need; I take care of them —" And yet children many times don't feel loved. They say, "My parents only love me when I get good grades, or when I get dressed by myself, or when I keep my room clean. When I'm good, they love me; the other times, no!" These children don't perceive that they are loved as individuals, uncondionally, no strings attached. They feel that their parents love them conditionally. There is a danger in that kind of love.

It is quite easy to love an attractive, healthy, good-natured child. But not all children are born with these traits or have had the early experiences that mold them into lovable individuals. In fact, by the age of two, three, or four, some children have been treated in such a way that they seem to reject loving actions by negative behavior. The parent may not perceive that this negative behavior is actually a cry for love. A chain reaction may then take place and the parent will, in turn, tend to reject the unloving child. Parents must remember that the child who has a disagreeable temperament, is the one who most needs love, compassion and help. *The child who most tries our patience most needs our love.* The child who bites, steals, hits, or uses "bad" language may actually be testing you and asking unconsciously, "Can you really love me when I am so terrible?"

Other children react in just the opposite way. They could not possibly act in such "bad" ways for fear that they would be further rejected, so they do everything they can to be good.

The child who is overly anxious to please, at first may gain the desired result and receive extra attention and acceptance from others. But usually, it is not too long before this behavior gets on one's nerves and the child is brushed off without any explanation for this change in attitude. Rather than rejecting an overly solicitous child, it is better to take time to talk with him about his behavior. Make it very plain that you love him all the time, whether he is good or bad. Learning that you don't have to be good to be loved is an important lesson for children (and adults). To be loved and accepted because he or she exists is the right of every child. God loves each of us in this way. The least we can do is to show this same love to the children He has entrusted to our care.

Another type of child parents must be sure to fill with love is the one who withdraws from social interaction. This child can be the hardest to reach because he does not actively seek love and may even reject loving advances. One can never force love on anyone. Love is a gift that is freely given and that must be freely accepted. Through gentle, consistent behavior you can slowly win the trust and eventually the love of the withdrawn child, but this type of child may never be as cuddly or overly loving as another.

Some children, during various stages in their lives, may fluxuate from one type of behavior to another; from the negative to the overly pleasing, to the withdrawn. Loving your child through these stages is not easy, but is essential for your child's healthy personality growth.

Meeting your child's need for love, does not mean you ignore the need for discipline. It sometimes helps to realize that *behavior is caused*; that is, there is a reason for children's behaving the way they do. Understanding this important fact will help you not to take your child's rejection or undesirable behavior personally. It leaves you free to overlook the acute behavior and search for underlying causes and develop remedial strategies.

When you realize that there is a reason for obnoxious behavior, it is possible to divorce the objectionable behavior from the *"real" child who has a need to be loved.* You can then treat that child in an understanding and loving manner, even though he does not seem to deserve it. Filling your child's love cup may give him enough self-confidence to choose, on his own, to change or overcome objectionable behavior.

It is easy to empty a child's love cup. Without thinking we react to the negative, punish unjustly or hurt children's sensitive feelings with harsh words or actions. Many times we empty a child's love cup without realizing what we are doing. For example, the following actions are cup-emptying behaviors:

1. Expressing approval *only* when a child is good. To do so is to love a child conditionally.

2. Threatening a child in an attempt to correct him.

3. Expressing a critical attitude.

4. Screaming or yelling at a child.

5. Expressing by words or looks, your disappointment or disgust.

6. Giving the "silent treatment."

7. Being too busy to give attention.

8. Using a child's name in a negative manner.

Yes, it is easy to empty a child's love cup, and every parent is guilty of an occasional mistake. But don't be overcome with guilt. Just be willing to say "I'm sorry," and then begin the filling process. Here's how:

First, *show acceptance* by respecting each child as an individual with God-given personality traits even when they may at times be hidden by some very unlovely behavior. Attempt to understand. Let your child know that he is wanted and welcome. Love unconditionally.

Second, *listen carefully to your child,* even if your

child has some very unlovely things to say. And listen to his body language. Many times children don't express in words how they are feeling, but they act out their feelings. Create a comfortable and warm atmosphere where your child feels free to express himself.

Third, *spend time with your child*, not just when you have time to spend, but whenever your child needs you, even though it may be a most inopportune time, such as when the baby's crying or you're on the telephone. Obviously, one cannot drop everything every time a child needs attention. For example, if your child comes to you with his needs at a time when you can't meet them immediately, don't rudely brush him off with, "Can't you see I'm busy?" Try giving him a quick hug or a loving smile and say pleasantly, "I'm busy right now, honey, but as soon as I can, I'll listen to what you want to tell me."

Children need to learn patience and understanding of others, but far too often adults tend to put their own priorities above that of their children. If children are suffering from an empty love cup, this tendency to neglect individual attention could be read by them as further rejection.

Let each child know that you enjoy being with him. You can communicate this message by cuddling, holding, hugging and touching when appropriate. It's by meeting a child's physical and emotional needs, through the time you spend together, that best says, "I love you."

Children Need to Be TRUSTED

The first year of your child's life is the critical time for him to develop trust (or faith) in his parents and/or his primary caregivers. If the care and attention he receives is loving and consistent and his physical needs are met, then trust is a natural outgrowth. As a child develops, he not only needs to be able to trust his environment, but he also needs to have an ever-increasing amount of trust placed in him. So often we forget that trust is a two-way street. Parents must not only be trustworthy, but must also show that they trust their child.

Why does a child need to be trusted?

First of all, trust is essential if children are to be taught to think through problems for themselves (seeking help and advice when needed) and then make their own decisions. Too often parents feel that they should make all decisions for young children, since adults know what is best. But when their children have grown older, they wonder why they have a difficult time making decisions by themselves or end up making decisions that are not clearly thought through. The only way one learns to make good decisions is through the experience of taking part in the decision-making process. If your child is going to gain this experience, you must show that you *trust* him to make age-appropriate decisions.

The second reason a child needs to be trusted is because it is through trust that a child learns to be responsible. Teachers can "teach" children many things, but it is not until children are given a chance to use knowledge that the instructors know how effective their teaching has been. If you, as a parent, consistently make all the decisions for your child, tell him what to do, go with him to make sure it is done, and criticize him for minor errors while carrying out a task, your child will never have a chance to demonstrate his skills and knowledge. He then may develop a feeling of uncertainty concerning his ability to carry responsibility. It is often safer for him to shun responsibility than to take it, if he knows that his mom or dad doesn't completely trust him. Adults are often very surprised at how responsible children are and how responsibly they act when they know they are trusted. Children respond to trust and will try their very best not to disappoint the person who does trust them.

An exciting example of how children respond to trust comes from a student attending a private school which specializes in the education and rehabilitation of incorrigible children. An eleven-year-old girl acted as guide for a tour group visiting the school. The visitors were impressed with the way she conducted the tour.

One of the men in the group expressed to the school director his pleasure. "That girl is wonderful," he said. "She is so responsible! She has so many good things to say about the school!"

"Two weeks ago," the director said, "that girl was sent to me after being kicked out of school for the eighth time. Incorrigible. Yet we trusted her with being a tour director and perhaps for the first time in her life she was challenged by the trust placed in her, and she has responded with responsible behavior."

Parents often feel that they should tell children every answer and solve all their problems. They don't realize that at a very early age children can learn to find their own answers, solve their own problems, and plan their own learning activities. The earlier the child can take this responsibility for his learning, the more progress he will be able to make. It is also true that an older child, or a child who has just learned a certain concept, might be the better teacher for a faltering child than an adult. Allowing a child to teach is a good way to show your trust in and the confidence you have in his skills and abilities.

Trust is also important to help children learn responsibility for their behavior. For example, if you expect your children to be noisy and rough, they will usually reward this expectation. Yet, if your children are given adequate information about what will be happening, and you explain how you need their cooperation, even the youngest child will usually do his best to reward your trust.

The third important reason why children need to be trusted is that trust shows the parent's confidence in them as individuals, which, in turn, bolsters their own confidence. It is true that children must learn to be dependent upon God, and, in many situations, to depend on others around them; but at the same time children must learn how to do many things for themselves. From infancy children should be encouraged to do those things which are appropriate for their age and ability. In other words, you should encourage your children to become more independent. Children must feel good about themselves and confident in their abilities to be successfully independent, and without trust this is almost impossible.

The following are some ideas about what parents can do to show their children they are trusted:

For the one-year-old:

Encourage independence in eating.

Encourage him to follow simple directions.

Ask him to hand you certain objects.

For the two-year-old:

Encourage independence in dressing, toileting and bathing by saying, "You can do it by yourself."

Show appreciation and approval when your child shows initiative in accomplishing a task on his own.

Let him participate in group activities.

For the three-year-old:

Talk to him and listen to what he has to say — and believe him.

Let him answer questions. (You should not do all the talking.)

Ask him what he would like to do.

Ask him what songs he would like to sing.

Ask him to pray.

Expect him to behave in appropriate ways.

For the four-year-old:

Let him teach other children.

Encourage him to solve his own problems, whether they are intellectual or social.

Encourage him to draw his own pictures or make his own creative work.

Let him run simple errands.

For the five-year-old:

Say, "I know you don't want to do it, but I need help and I know that I can trust you to help me out when I need it."

Let him sing songs and tell stories that he composes.

Let him plan, carry out and evaluate his learning experiencies.

A parent's trust helps children develop the ability to make decisions and become responsible and self-confident individuals. In addition, it can be an example to them of God's trust in His children. For as you trust your children to follow what you say, so does their heavenly Father trust them to follow what He has said in His Bible. It is the child's responsibility to fulfill this trust. No one else can make that decision for him.

Children Need to Be FREE to Experience Life

Children must experience life in order to learn. They must move, explore, express themselves and play.

An old Chinese proverb states,
When I hear, I forget.
When I see, I remember.
When I do, I learn.

Children at every age must be free to become actively involved in the learning process. Learning, for children, does not mean sitting back and merely listening and looking; it means moving, exploring, creating, expressing and playing. But it is only in an environment where the child feels relatively free that this type of learning can occur. To develop this feeling of freedom (freedom which leads to learning) a very young child needs, not only a physically safe environment where he is not afraid he will get injured when he runs, jumps, climbs and explores, but also a psychologically safe environment where he is not afraid of criticism and censure.

In order to meet your child's needs for freedom, make sure of the following: First, your home and yard must be safe for children's play. Second, you should be the kind of individual that fosters your child's sense of well-being and security — a person capable of protecting him from physical as well as psychological injury. Do not allow harsh words, name-calling, tattling, accusations and criticism to be expressed among children.

Children need to move. Children, especially young children, learn through their movements. Developing a good foundation in the physical skills has proved to be an important prerequisite for learning more formal academic skills such as reading.

Before your child starts first grade, he should have experienced a large variety of movement activities designed to develop motor skills. In fact, your child should be able to do the following:

1. Run in a coordinated manner without bumping into obstacles.

2. Gallop, skip, hop, jump.
3. Balance while standing on one foot.

4. Hit a large target by throwing a ball underhand or overhand.

5. Draw a circle, a square, a triangle, a rectangle.

6. Dress himself, including front buttons and other reachable fasteners.

7. Tie shoelaces.

At the beginning of first grade, a child may not be able to do all these things perfectly, but he should be moving toward gaining control of his movements. Movement skills must come before more advanced cognitive learning. Without the freedom (and encouragement) to practice these skills during his preschool years, your child will be handicapped when entering a more academic school program.

Relations with other children may also suffer if movement skills are poor. Peers tend to make fun of the awkward child who can't pump a swing, ride a tricycle or climb a tree like the rest.

Children need to explore. Just as the young child's body is active, so is his mind. He is curious; he wants to find out how things work, where things are and how they feel. Combining your child's need for movement with his need to know will lead to exploratory behavior.

Burton L. White,[1] a foremost authority on the child from birth to three, suggests that curiosity is one behavior that is at high risk during these years because parents do not realize its value.

When crawlers are continually kept in the confines of a playpen merely for the parents' convenience, they are too limited in their exploration. When toddlers are kept indoors for fear they will get dirty or fall down and hurt themselves, their exploration is too contained. When your child is always told "Don't touch," or when the objects he does get hold of are immediately taken from him, he becomes frustrated in his desire to know, and he is prevented from developing the mental frame necessary for later abstract thinking. He is likely to react in one of two ways.

First, he may explore on the sly, touching forbidden objects and going to forbidden places when your back is turned. This can lead to deceitfulness and possible injury because of lack of supervision. It is much better to say to the curious child, "Let me hold it while you touch it," or "If you want to see what is outside the fence, I'll go with you." Or, just put away valuables your child shouldn't touch.

The second possible reaction your child may have if he's not allowed to explore is that he may obey your message and inhibit his desire to explore. This, however, may effect his academic success in school. Exploratory behavior is important for learning.

When the child who reacts in this way reaches preschool or first grade, he may be afraid to explore his environment even though inwardly he may be curious. A child learns through curiosity and exploration. Therefore, all children should be encouraged to look, taste, manipulate, feel, smell, listen, ask questions and talk about their findings. In order to foster curiosity, you must be convinced that exploratory behavior is important and that a child learns through his unstructured, random explorations. You will then design the environment in such a way as to encourage a child's curiosity. Here are some suggestions.

1. Children should be given freedom to explore without having the fear of destroying fragile materials or having you censor every move. In order to feel secure, safe and free to explore, children need reasonable limits as guidelines for their behavior. (See Chapter 4 — under "Define limits," page 90.) They then know what is acceptable and can explore freely and safely.

2. There should be enough adult supervision so that children can be free to be curious with the materials and environment, but there should not be so much supervision that children feel inhibited.

3. A variety of attractive, provocative and safe toys and objects should be provided. These do not need to be expensive "educational toys," but objects that the children have not had an opportunity to see or handle before. Try, for example, manipulative tools, such as a level or a blunt-nozzle oil can. Common household items such as jar rings or clothespins make great toys for young children. Even fruits and vegetables such as broccoli, brussel sprouts, artichokes, avocados or pineapples are interesting and often unusual objects to a child. Objects that encourage a child to use his senses are good for stimulating curiosity. For example, for smell, try a lemon, perfume, or even horseradish; for taste, try cloves, garlic, ginger or other herbs; for hearing, try objects that can produce different sounds, such as different lengths of pipe, bottles filled with water or gourds to shake; for feel, try sandpaper, sponges, fur or even a "surprise" box which daily contains a different object that your child may not look at but may only touch in order to identify.

4. Time must be allowed for exploratory behavior. If you plan every minute of your child's day with directed activities, it gives him no chance to pursue his own curiosity. Exploring takes time. Don't always let your time schedule interfere with your child's explorations. Instead of saying, "Come in for lunch right now," when your child is engrossed in watching a caterpillar eat a leaf, say, "When you are finished, you need to come in for lunch," or "Let's take it into the house while we eat lunch," or even, "Would you like to eat your lunch outside while you're watching the caterpillar?"

5. Stimulate your child's curiosity through challenging questions. The comment, "Look, the trees are growing leaves," will not stimulate as much curiosity as the comments, "The branches on this tree look different. I wonder why." "I wonder if we can pull a branch lower." "I wonder how it feels." "How does it smell? How does

it taste?" (Many common plants, such as oleander, are toxic. Because of the dangers of poisoning, caution your children never to taste anything unfamiliar unless they ask an informed adult.) Then children should be encouraged to talk about their discoveries.

Children need to express themselves. Children communicate through both words and actions. The younger the child, the more nonverbal communication he uses. But this does not mean his need to express himself is any less. It means that you, as a parent, must be more aware of your child's attempts to communicate; you must use more guesswork on the interpretation of what his actions mean. As children begin to use words, they are anxious to talk. The two- or three-year-old naturally finds it very, very difficult to keep quiet in places where keeping quiet is important, such as in church. But certainly in the home, keeping quiet does not necessarily mean that learning is taking place. In fact, the opposite may be true.

Children need to be talked to, they need to be listened to, and they need to be encouraged to express themselves. *They do not need a parent who talks all the time,* for children (and adults) retain only a small part of what they hear.

Children need to play. Adults often look at children's play as a nonproductive use of time. Because it may be fun, too many feel that play is not very useful. But play for a child is quite useful. It is through play that a child learns best. Play has been called the child's work. Certainly it is the child's learning laboratory. Through play the child learns about the world around him. He learns how to relate to people — his playmates and adults. He learns about adult roles (mother, father, teacher, minister, etc.), and he is able to test ideas and solve problems in a nonthreatening environment. Children also use play to act out experiences they have had and to internalize these experiences or come to terms with them.

Although play can be productive in an environment that has not been planned, the chance for beneficial results is increased significantly when parents provide a play environment that has been thoughtfully and carefully structured. Such planning should include not only the arrangement of the room and yard but also the provision of toys, materials and learning opportunities that will make it possible for each child to grow toward the specific objectives his parent's have made for him.

It takes time and freedom to play. Often parents plan so many adult-centered activities and lessons (horseback riding, gymnastics, piano, etc.) that very little time is left for the child to play with what he is really interested in.

If you choose a preschool experience for your child, you'll want to make sure play is a vital part of the curriculum. Many preschool teachers feel more secure when they are so completely in charge that all the children are doing the same thing. Then it is obvious when one child steps out of line. He can be easily and quickly corrected. However, when a variety of play experiences are going on at one time, the teacher's role is like that of a facilitator rather than a dictator. Through play, teaching can be individualized, meeting each child's level of understanding rather than just aiming for the middle of the group and missing both ends.

The idea that children should be free to experience life does not mean that they should not be appropriately taught, controlled, and disciplined. Quite the opposite. When children have *not* learned adequate behavior and self-control, appropriate restraints must be placed upon them for their own safety and the safety of other people and property.

When you, as parents, allow your children the necessary freedom to move, explore, create, express and play as a part of their daily experience, you will be meeting an important need in their lives.

Children Need to Be CHALLENGED

Young children enjoy repetition. They don't mind hearing their favorite stories and singing their favorite songs hundreds of times. But at the same time, when it comes to learning and to exhibiting appropriate behavior, children need a challenge. They don't like to be babied. They don't like to be treated as adults and have things expected of them as if they were much older. But they do like to be challenged.

Take, for example, your ten-year-olds who are very capable of washing the dishes. Do they enjoy washing dishes? It is probably not their favorite activity! Four-year-olds, however, usually love to wash the dishes. At four, washing the dishes is a real challenge. But because it is easier to do the dishes ourselves, we take this challenging task away from our children, and by the time they are old enough to do the job at our convenience, they don't want to.

Learning occurs most readily when two objectives are met: (1) The task you give your child should be simple enough so that he has the requisite skills to perform it without too much stress. (2) At the same time, the task should be difficult enough so he has to stretch his skills, knowledge or imagination to accomplish what needs to be done.

This delicate balance between the too-simple and the too-difficult provides the challenge that children need to make learning tasks and play situations growth-producing activities. When the challenge is present in learning opportunities, parents usually don't need to worry about motivation. Children learn for the joy of learning when the challenge is present. They don't need extra rewards. They don't need artificial motivation. They don't need to be pushed and prodded. Rather, they are eager to concentrate on the task at hand and conquer it.

When it comes to appropriate behavior, a challenge is also important. Children become frustrated when adults expect them to behave in ways that do not fit with their level of development. For example, frustration is inevitable when young children are required to sit for long periods of time without moving or expressing themselves. At the same time, children don't really want adults to allow them to act in ways that they know are not appropriate. They want strong adults who can help them to control their behavior so they can feel good rather than ashamed at what they have done.

Parents who are successful at offering a learning challenge to children have a way of letting each child know that they have high, yet realistic, expectations for that child, that they trust him to do his best and that they will be willing to help if the child needs it. They will also allow him to advance as rapidly as he is able. But, rather than encourage competition by his rapid advancement, they will encourage him to share his knowledge with his siblings and friends.

The family setting is an excellent opportunity to provide a challenge for children. Older children can be challenged to learn tasks well so they can teach the younger ones. At the same time, the younger child is challenged to learn skills like the older ones. Younger children learn by watching their older brothers and sisters. So, it is important to challenge your older children to behave in such a way as to be good examples.

There is perhaps no greater challenge for parents than to plan learning activities that have a built-in challenge for children.

Children Need to Be TAUGHT

Children cannot grow up like weeds, without proper cultivation and instruction, and be expected to be cultured and productive individuals. Children need to be molded, trained, influenced and educated. Children need to be taught the way they should go.

In order for parents to understand what and how they should be teaching children, they need to know the characteristics of young children's thinking. Children don't think the way adults do.

What are the characteristics of a young child's thinking? Here are four:

1. *Thinking is egocentric.* The younger the child the more he lacks an awareness of anything outside of his own immediate experience. For example, infants, at first, are unaware that their own hands and feet are a part of their bodies. They also do not realize that objects exist when they can no longer be seen. Egocentric thinking persists throughout early childhood and affects a child in the following ways:

He does not realize that his thoughts or actions make up part of the situation in which he is involved.

He is not able to understand situations by looking at another person's point of view.

He has difficulty imagining how it would be if he were someone else.

He cannot view himself from the angle of somebody else.

He cannot pretend to be another person and still be himself. Through fantasy he can pretend, but it is difficult to put himself into the picture at the same time.

He cannot see his own and other's points of view at the same time.

He sees inanimate objects as alive — just as he is alive.

Furthermore, the young child doesn't realize that adults can't tell what is going on inside of him. If he hears ringing in his ears, he thinks others should hear it too. When he answers the telephone and Grandmother on the other end asks, "Who is this?" he answers, "It's me." Then he can't understand why Grandmother persists, "But who is *me*?"

2. *Thinking is dominated by perceptions.* The young child is greatly influenced by what he sees, hears or otherwise experiences at a given moment. For him, "Seeing is believing." He seldom pays attention to subtle changes from one state to another; rather he sees things as static — as standing still. Young children do not use their past experience as a basis for reasoning. If they "see" something happening, even though they may never have seen it before, they believe it is true. This is why young children believe a magician really can find a rabbit in an empty hat, or they insist something is true because they have seen it on television.

3. *Thinking is from the particular to the particular, rather than from general to particular.* The young child must grow to understand that events are caused and situations differ. They don't understand the fact that when something happens in one situation it does not mean it will happen the same way in every situation. An example of this type of naive reasoning is illustrated when a child says, "Billy rode a bicycle. Why can't I?" The child does not realize that there may be many factors in Billy's situation that are different from those in his own. Only through experience does the child begin to realize that his behavior will in a large part determine how he is treated.

4. *Thinking is relatively unsocialized.* As children grow older, they become more aware of the people around them. They begin to pay more attention to what others say and how they think. Young children, however, who are still very egocentric, pay very little attention. They do not feel that they have to justify their conclusions to anyone. They think everyone should know what they think about and how they have arrived at certain conclusions. Even if they try to reconstruct their thought process to show another person how they

have arrived at a decision, they find it most difficult, if not impossible. This is the reason that the question "Why did you do it?" has very little meaning for a child. He may very well respond truthfully with an "I don't know" or a "Because" and a shrug of the shoulders. As a child becomes aware of himself as a thinker, and as he is able to think about a number of different aspects of a situation at the same time, he will begin to adjust his thinking to that of other people. It takes many years of interaction — discussing, arguing, agreeing and disagreeing — before a child learns the ground rules necessary for logical thinking.

A prerequisite to effective teaching is for you, as parents, to clearly understand what you want your children to learn. Plans should include long-range general goals such as "an understanding of God's plan for their lives" or "more appropriate behavior." Goals establish a general direction for child rearing, but daily effectiveness is enhanced by immediate objectives for specific children, such as "for Johnny to learn where Genesis is in the Bible" or "for Mary to wash her hands before lunch."

"Specific learning objectives" is terminology which is usually applied to the classroom rather than the home environment. But parents can increase their effectiveness by writing daily learning objectives for each child. Objectives should include the physical, mental and spiritual development of the child.

Physical Objectives: Physical objectives are those objectives that are related to a child's physical-motor growth and development. Learning to walk, run, hop, skip, roller-skate, jump rope, print letters and write first names are all important physical-motor skills that your preschool child should learn. (See Chapter 2 under "Activity.")

Mental Objectives: These objectives have to do with the child's cognitive learning such as understanding facts about nature and scientific discoveries, learning names for objects, solving problems and learning academic skills that help to prepare your child for later success in such school subjects as reading, science and mathematics. Objectives such as the following would be appropriate for preschool children: (1) To identify a rose from a group of five different flowers. (2) To recognize his name when printed on a card. (3) To compare objects that sink with those that float.

One of the most important things that you can do to help your young child develop mentally is to sharpen his perception. This can be facilitated in the following ways:

1. There must be time provided to experiment with materials, to find out how they work and to discover how they are different from other materials. For example, let your child discover the differences and similarities between ice and water.

2. Help your child to use all of his senses to find out about materials. For example, for feeling, provide two each of different types of materials or fabric which the child, blindfolded, can match to those that have the same feel. For hearing, provide different objects that can be put in non-see-through containers (two of rice, two of dried beans, two of pebbles, etc.). The child can shake the containers and then match those that sound alike. For tasting, provide different materials that have a distinctive taste, something sweet, something sour, something salty and something bitter. Your child can taste them and then talk about their differences. For smelling, provide different things that have an identifiable smell, such as onions, roses or fresh-cut grass. Your child can smell these and talk about their differences. For seeing, show your child a large picture and ask him to point to smaller objects in the picture. Provide magnifying glasses so that your children can see more easily the parts of an object.

Provide a variety of materials for his discrimination. Sand, water, clay, playdough and mud are all good experimental materials for your child.

3. Ask your child to point out similarities and differences in materials and objects. For example: "How are these objects the same?" "Find one just like this one." Matching games such as lotto or dominoes may be helpful. You can also have your child look for certain characteristics in objects. For example: "Find the red fork." "Find the pencil with an eraser on it." "Bring me a block that looks just like this one." For another discrimination activity, place a variety of objects on a table and have your child find the object you ask for or find the object just like the one you show him.

4. Stimulate your child to think logically. For example: "If you do this, what will happen?" "Why does this happen?"

5. Be an example. Wherever you go with your child, be perceptive of the surroundings. Notice little things and draw them to his attention, such as the ants walking in a line, the smell of a rose or the song of a bird.

6. Encourage experimentation by using the scientific method.

When children are confronted with a problem, rather than guessing at a solution in a random, hit-or-miss fashion, logical thinking is enhanced when they follow the scientific method. This method includes (1) forming a hypothesis, (2) planning an experiment to test the hypothesis, (3) performing the experiment and obtaining the results, (4) drawing the conclusion from the results, and (5) forming a new hypothesis if the answer to the problem is still unknown.

For example, let's say one of your children notices that the plants in the room face toward the window. Rather than having him guess why this is happening and then telling him why a certain answer is correct, you can encourage your child to test out each different reason in the scientific way and logically come up with the best answer.

Spiritual Objectives: Spiritual objectives are of primary importance. These include objectives about your child's relationship to God and to others.

First, consider your children's relationship to God. Even young children can be taught that God created all things, including themselves, as an expression of His love. They need to be taught about Jesus, their special Friend and Brother who now lives in heaven, and about God, who is not only Jesus' Father, but their very own heavenly Father too. They need to know and understand God's and Jesus' love and care for them in the little things that happen each day. They need to understand that God has a plan for their lives. If adults don't point out these things to children and make them aware of God's continual presence, children may not perceive this. A knowledge of God's love and Jesus' sacrifice for them and the presence of God's Spirit and the angels can be a tremendous comfort to a child when he is discouraged, alone or lost. It can give him the faith he needs to develop in every aspect of his life. Parents, you must take advantage of every opportunity to make God real to your children in such a way that your children develop complete love and trust in God, rather than obey His commandments because of fear. To help your chldren gain this concept say such things as these:

1. "Your angel is always with you wherever you go."

2. "Jesus loves all children."

3. "God takes care of His children as He took care of Jesus in the wilderness when He sent angels to feed Him."

Don't say to your child:

1. "You'd better not do that, or your angel will see you and write it down."

2. "Jesus won't love you if you do that."

3. "If you're not good, God won't give you what you ask for."

4. "If you're naughty you won't go to heaven."

The second aspect of a child's spiritual development is the child's relationship to others. It is the character of an individual that determines how he relates to other people. Children need to be taught the importance of developing beautiful characters while they are yet small. In fact, character building is probably the most important work ever entrusted to human beings. Character is developed early and remains fairly stable throughout life. What character traits should children develop in the early years that will enhance their relationship to their peers, siblings, parents and other adults?

Although a list of desirable character traits could go on for pages, the Bible contains a number of lists of selected traits that appear to be especially important for the basic character development curriculum for young children.

2 Peter 1:5-7	Galatians 5:22,23	Philippians 4:8	Matthew 5:3-12
Faith	Love	True	Poor in spirit
Virtue	Joy	Honest	Meek
Knowledge	Peace	Just	Merciful
Temperance	Longsuffering	Pure	Pure in heart
Patience	Gentleness	Lovely	Peacemakers
Godliness	Goodness	Good report	
Brotherly kindness	Faith		
Charity	Meekness		
	Temperance		

Children need many things, but most of all, children need understanding parents — parents who exhibit the following characteristics:

1. Parents who give special TIME to each child. Time is a precious talent and when it is given to children, it is never lost. Good quality time, willingly invested in young children where parents show acceptance and are willing to listen, will meet their children's need for love.

2. Parents who UNDERSTAND children's individual and age characteristics. Parents should not expect too much or too little, but place the appropriate amount of *trust* in each individual child. The successful parent will allow each child to make choices and carry responsibilities that are appropriate for his age level.

3. Parents who are CONSISTENT in what they require of children and STRONG enough to enforce basic requirements. Parents who are consistent and have a strength of character are usually highly respected for what they stand for. They can, at the same time, allow their children more freedom to move, explore, express themselves and play because they are in "planned" control of the home environment.

4. Parents who ENCOURAGE children. Children are sensitive and can be easily discouraged if they constantly meet with failure and censure. However, with encouragement, each child can be led to meet the *challenge* of the tasks around him with assurance, interest and enthusiasm.

5. Parents who KNOW CHRIST PERSONALLY. This type of parent will not only teach children through precept but, more important, by the example of his own life. By sharing his personal Christian experience with his children he can be instrumental in teaching them values far beyond the secular environment. The parent who knows Christ personally will willingly fulfill the responsibility God has placed upon him or her to be the first and most important teacher of the child in every aspect of life.

In summary, you might think of understanding the basic needs of all children as the star that will guide you in a deeper understanding of your child.

The five points of the star correspond to a child's five basic needs: (1) to be loved, (2) to be trusted, (3) to be free to experience life, (4) to be challenged, (5) to be taught.

The inner area of the star represents the type of parent each child needs to help him meet these basic needs:

1. The need to be loved requires a parent who willingly gives time to each child.

2. The need to be trusted requires a parent who has an understanding of the individual and age characteristics of children.

3. The need to be free to experience life requires a parent who is consistent and strong enough to allow the child freedom within a planned environment.

4. The need to be challenged requires a parent who will encourage children to do their best.

5. The need to be taught requires a parent who knows Christ personally and who will encourage the child to develop his own relationship with God.

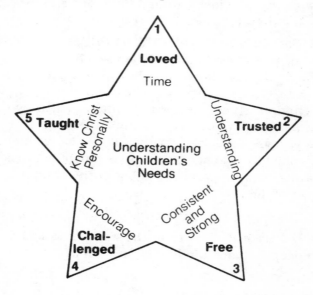

Good understanding wins favor . . .
Prov. 13:15 NIV

Understanding
Individual Characteristics

Every child is unique. Travel the world over and you won't find two exactly alike — not even identical twins. What a challenge to attempt to understand each child's individual characteristics and at the same time accept each child just the way he is. Accepting, however, doesn't mean you shouldn't thoughtfully and gently attempt to mold his behavior into habit patterns which will help him develop to his true potential.

You've seen the bumper sticker, "To know me is to love me." Well, we all know this isn't necessarily so. Some children's undesirable characteristics have the opposite effect. Instead of being drawn to them, we are repulsed. Parents must realize that every child goes through stages where negative behavior and obnoxious attitudes tend to dominate. Look at the adjectives that child psychology books use to describe the typical two- to four-year-old: selfish, stubborn, destructive, egocentric, negative, unruly. These are definitely not desirable characteristics; they are immature behaviors. The challenge is to get to know and understand why children are acting this way so changes can be made. Understanding makes it possible to treat children in a loving manner in spite of their negative traits. You can learn how to make the words of the bumper sticker, "To know me is to love me," come true in the life of your child!

Let's start this process by noting how children differ at birth. Nine specific characteristics have been noted:[2]

1. *Activity level:* Some children are never still from morning till night; others are sluggish and slow.

2. *Regularity of bodily function:* Some babies eat every four hours on the dot and sleep through the night at three months of age; for others, parents can never count on them to do the same things twice! Beware! Toilet training may take twice as long with an "irregular" toddler!

3. *Approach or withdrawal as a characteristic response to a new situation:* Some children jump into new things, others become rigid, draw away, or cry.

4. *Adaptability to change in routine:* Some children adapt to any situation; others cannot tolerate the slightest change.

5. *Level of sensory threshold:* Some babies can sleep through earthquake or thunder; some wake at the drop of a pin.

6. *Positive or negative mood:* Some have a naturally sunny disposition; others seem to have been born on the wrong side of the delivery table!

7. *Intensity of response:* Some babies whine gently when hungry; others scream their heads off.

8. *Distractability:* Some children are distracted by any disturbance; others persist through thick and thin!

9. *Persistence and attention span:* Believe it or not, some children are able to sit still and stay tuned in throughout the church service; others are ready to leave halfway through the opening prayer!

Children are different! Your friends who give all the child-rearing advice probably have been blessed with children who are fairly easy to live with; who are quiet, regular, adaptable, positive, and persistent. But I would venture a guess that most of you who are reading this book have bumped up against some rather difficult-to-live-with characteristics in your child and you are earnestly searching for some answers. This chapter is for you. The key is to get to know the disposition of your child. As you recognize his or her faults, you will be able to *encourage the opposite behaviors.* Practical suggestions are given for encouraging the following traits: activity, self-control, adaptability, tranquility, positive mood, approachability, persistence, creativity, and generosity.

Activity vs. Nonactivity

Some children are much more active than others. They need many opportunities to run, climb, jump and wiggle. These children are often called "troublemakers" in church or in group situations, not because they want to cause trouble, but because the adult may have set up a situation that is incompatible with their natural need for movement. It is impossible for this type of child to sit still for a very long time without undue tension and frustration.

Through activity a child strengthens his muscles and builds a healthy body. Parents err when they forget how important it is for a child to have freedom to move, not just in the house, but in large wide-open spaces. They err when they feel that children are learning only when they are sitting quietly and listening to the TV or a teacher. We now know from psychologists and sophisticated research studies that a young child learns best through his body movement, for this is the way that he not only discovers his world, but the way he organizes this information into useful knowledge.[3]

Most parents and teachers will admit that the quiet, nonactive child is a great deal easier to work with.

Because it is tiring to work with extremely active children all day, many parents try to restrict a child's activity by placing him in a playpen or in front of the television for long periods of time. These "trained" children, and others who are naturally less active, may need to be encouraged to be more active. This can be done in a number of ways.

1. Alternate active and nonactive activities. For example, after a story encourage your child to get up and act it out or go outside.

2. The younger the child, the greater is the need for freedom and spontaneous activity. Younger children often have a more difficult time holding still or staying with the same activity than do older children. And because boys mature more slowly than girls, they appear to need more physical activity.

3. Encourage active games. Ask, for example, "How long can you hop on one foot?" Create an obstacle course for your child to run through. Time a child as he runs a certain distance and see if he can beat his own record. Jumping rope is a great exercise that even many three-year-olds can learn. A child can learn to count while trying to beat his own endurance record.

4. Give your children information on how activity makes their bodies grow. When they are using certain muscles, mention how the muscles are growing and getting stronger because they are using them. Have them run or jump until they can feel their hearts beating (don't overdo this) and talk about how exercise keeps their hearts strong.

5. Encourage exercising and jogging. Taking a daily jogging trip around the block will not only be a special treat but will also improve the health of both you and your child. You can also do daily exercises with your child. Keep these exercises simple, and you'll find that your child will enjoy copying your motions. The jogging and exercise habit is a good one to establish early in life.

Some children appear to be overly active or active at the "wrong" time. A child should not be disciplined for something he has very little control over, such as his need for activity. The parent must be observant enough to recognize this need and plan for it. For example, this may mean that family worship, where the whole family participates, will last only a few minutes (five at the most) and then your more active child should have the option of whether he wants to stay for a story and songs or not. This would be much wiser planning than requiring a super-active child to sit for a long time and end up having his behavior disrupt everyone's worship experience. Punishing him in this situation could lead to an early dislike of worship situations, just the opposite of the attitude you are trying to foster.

Nap time is usually difficult for children with a high activity level. You can make it easier for a child to rest if there are as few distractions as possible. You might give the child a book to look at while resting and don't expect him to nap as long as your other children. In addition to nap time, active young children may need short rest periods throughout the day.

What about hyperactivity? What one parent might term hyperactivity, another might see as normal, but very active behavior. Even professionals sometimes disagree on the diagnosis. It is best if active children aren't tagged with a diagnosis that labels them different from others and then treated as though they have a dreadful disease! Sometimes medication is necessary to slow a child down long enough so that the significant others in his life can begin giving him positive strokes instead of continual punishment. But scientists don't yet know the long-term effects of medication or what it does to a child's ability to learn.

A good diet is of vital importance for the child with hyperactive tendencies. A diet free from artificial flavoring, sugar, refined foods and preservatives,[4] of course, helps every child — hyperactive or not. The most important thing it does for the active child is shift the focus of blame from the child to the diet and allows his family and friends to begin to see him more positively.

Parents should also try to control excessive stimulation. Monitor loud music and wild T.V. shows. Avoid florescent colors and lights. Put up unnecessary toys and clean up the clutter.

The very active child is usually not a significant problem to flexible parents who allow him the freedom he needs in a safe environment and have time to keep a close eye on his activities so the house isn't torn apart. Parents of hyperactive children need a good support system, so they can take an occasional break and come back to their parenting task with renewed energy and creative ideas.

The biggest problem usually surfaces when the hyperactive child starts school. Regular classrooms with one teacher and 25-30 students aren't designed for children who have a difficult time sitting still and listening. Parents should consider keeping these children home for an extra year or so until they are better able to handle the structure of formal schooling, or they should look for a program that meets their child's special needs.

A child who has been professionally diagnosed as hyperactive often exhibits related behaviors that are disturbing: difficulty making decisions, absent-mindedness, short memory, difficulty listening and following through with requests, disorganization and the need for immediate gratification. Here are some helpful suggestions:

1. Be firm and establish clear ground rules.

2. Don't flood your child with petty time-consuming decisions. If your child dawdles and shows indecisiveness over such things as what to wear or what

to clean up first, you make the choice.

3. Don't haggle over small things. Children can often exhibit great control over situations by arguing about insignificant things. You should make a decision, even if it's in error and not allow your child to fall into the habit of haggling. Have faith in yourself.

4. Do give your hyperactive child chores to do. But select one or two and be prepared for the fact that it will take time, effort, goodwill and many calm reminders to get these chores done.

5. Be prepared for your child's absent-mindedness. Very active children often need reminders, but avoid getting irritated and saying, "I've told you a million times." Patiently keep on your child's case until the job is done. Short lists help. They're impersonal and your child will gain satisfaction as he checks off tasks completed.

6. Be sure your child hears you and understands what you have said. Get his attention — look in his eyes and make your request in slow deliberate language. It's not a bad idea to have him repeat the request, just to make sure he understands.

7. If your child tends to be disorganized in his thinking and behavior, you may have to calmly ask "who, what, where and when" questions to get the necessary information.

8. Teach your child manners. Hyperactive children can learn to wait for their turn and not interrupt others. Use your common sense. If you can fulfill his needs, do so, but if you feel this behavior is abnormally disruptive you must correct him firmly. Don't let your child be unduly loud and noisy in a public place. Do something about it quickly even if it is embarrassing. Saying, "Just wait till I get you home" doesn't help this type of child!

9. Help others to understand your child's difficulties. Don't down-grade your child in front of others, nor should you make excuses, so your child feels he can get

by with obnoxious behavior. Instruct others how best to work with your child.

10. Children don't always grow out of these hyperactive tendencies and the related behaviors. But as they mature they will learn effective ways to cope with their behavior. The most important thing is that a child, despite his handicaps, feels accepted and valued.

When it comes to hyperactivity, the most important thing you can give your child is your understanding attitude. You must take what some might consider a handicap and help turn it into an asset. Active grown-ups are in high demand!

Self-Control vs. Impulsivity

An impulsive child is not able to control his actions when the task he is working on demands this control. He is the one who seems to jump into things without thinking, leaves tasks partially finished in order to begin something new, and may act inappropriately in certain social situations.

Impulsivity is a characteristic of most young children because their thinking has not yet matured enough to think clearly from cause to effect and consider consequences. They cannot think through what the results of their behavior or words might be. Therefore, a thought and the corresponding action occurs almost instantaneously.

Very young children have a difficult time controlling their movements and are bumping into furniture, beating the drum ten times when the parent says three, and scribbling rather than drawing controlled lines. But by four years of age the child should be gaining control over some of these behaviors. If a child continues to be impulsive, this can interfere with his learning and will probably cause problems for him in his social relationships.

To help a child gain control over his impulses, you must have enough time to give individual attention as he needs it. Looking for the cause of your child's impulsivity may give you clues on how to work with him. He may be tired or hungry. He may even be ill. He may become frustrated easily. He may feel insecure or afraid. Or he may be only copying the behavior he has seen in his home or among his friends. You can then plan activities that will meet his specific needs. For example, if your child is frustrated by working on small materials, you can guide him into large muscle activity. If a child is becoming overly excited in noisy, active play, you can help him find a quiet activity which he will enjoy for a while before going back to his active play.

The following activities may help the impulsive child to gain further control over his movements:

Games:

1. Water pouring. Paint lines on clear plastic containers that you can see through. Your child can practice pouring the water and stopping when it reaches a certain line (A line drawn in red fingernail polish on the container will stick well to plastic.) Water tinted with food coloring may be easier for the child to see.

2. Ball rolling. Draw lines or place strings across a sidewalk at different distances from your child. Have him roll balls and try to get them to stop on the different lines.

3. Games like "Red light — Green light." Have your child run or walk when you say, "Green light." Then when you say, "Red light" have him practice stopping his movements.

Music activities:

1. Allow your child to play rhythm instruments to different types of music. Encourage him to change from fast to slow, from loud to soft, and from an uneven to an even rhythm as the music changes. Example: "Tell

me if the music sounds different." "How is it different?"

2. Play the strings of an autoharp from low to high and back. Your child can move his hands or feet (while lying down) in the direction of the sound of the music. After doing this for a number of times, continue playing slowly in the middle range to see if he can stop his hands or feet half way up or down.

Body movement activities:

1. Ice-cream cone. Have your child pretend that he is an ice-cream cone. Suggest that he add scoops of ice cream and then stretch as tall as he can. Pretend he goes out into the sun and begins to melt, very slowly, until he is a puddle of milk on the floor.

2. Popcorn. Have your child be a kernel of corn. Pretend to turn on the popcorn popper and encourage him to wait as the pan gets hotter and hotter until you say it is time to "pop."

3. Jack-in-the-box. Have your child pretend that he is a jack-in-the-box and must wait inside the box until you say "Jump!"

4. Rising sun. Talk about how slowly the sun rises and moves across the sky. Then say, "If you were the sun, how would you come up?" Encourage your child to move slowly to the sound of music.

5. Growing flower. Act out the flower slowly pushing out of the soil and growing leaves.

Learning to control impulsive movements is just one aspect of self-control that children must develop. It is also important for children to develop control of their words, which often has to do with handling their emotions (See Chapter 3). The young child's need for immediate gratification might also be considered a type of impulsive behavior. As children learn to think beyond themselves and consider other's opinions and needs, their need for immediate personal gratification is diminished (See the section on generosity in this chapter.).

Adaptability vs. Rigidity

The adaptable child, no matter what his initial reaction to something might be, soon adjusts to the situation. Other children may react very strongly to change, and it takes them a great deal of time to get used to a new situation. The more rigid child will be upset by even slight changes in the home (such as rearrangement of the furniture), or the daily schedule (such as a trip to the zoo), or even a change in mother's hairstyle.

As children grow older, they become more adaptable. Adaptability is not something that can always be taught; it is something that has to be grown into. Time is the answer. If you have a child who adapts slowly, take the extra effort to warn him that changes are coming. For example, when a mother knows she must be absent the following day, she can tell her child about this, talk about the babysitter who will be staying with him, help him to learn her name, or ask him to help the sitter to find where certain things are.

Not all changes can be anticipated. When the unexpected happens, the rigid child can be helped to adjust by just being close to you or a trusted adult and gaining reassurance through this closeness. It is not enough for these children to be told, "You don't need to be afraid or upset, just because things are different today." These comments just disregard your child's right to have feelings.

It is much better to accept these feelings and deal with them directly, since to your child the feelings are very real. You could say, "I know you are upset that your best friend could not come over today, but Mary is playing house and there's an extra doll for you." Then you can ask for Mary's cooperation by saying, "Mary, Jill is feeling bad today because her friend Kelly is not here. Could you play dolls with her so she won't feel lonesome?"

It may not always work. But it's worth a try. And it is certainly much better than disregarding a child's right to have feelings.

Tranquility vs. Intensity

Children differ in the intensity of their reactions to different situations. When someone announces a surprise to a group of children, some will jump up and down and clap their hands; others will sit still and say "Goody;" some will smile, while others retain a placid expresion on their faces. The child who is intense in his feelings reacts more strongly to positive things as well as the negative. This child is also more sensitive to praise as well as criticism. When this child needs to be corrected, a glance in his direction is often enough, while with a less intense child more action would be needed.

You can often learn about how your children are reacting to a certain story or situation by watching the facial expressions of your most responsive, intense child. For example, in a thunderstorm the intense child is more likely to show his feelings of fear, or when an aquarium fish dies, show his feelings of sorrow. You can then say something to help all the children cope with the situation realistically.

When you know a certain child will react more intensely, an effort should be made to plan the day in such a way so that child is not exposed to an overabundance of exciting and stimulating activities, materials or T.V.

Even Bible stories like David and Goliath or Daniel and the Lion's Den may be too scary and exciting for the intense child to handle. Children are different and we must respect these differences. Over-excitement is not good for children since it interferes with the necessary pattern of eating, resting, and learning. The atmosphere of a Christian home should be one of peace and restfulness.

Positive vs. Negative Mood

Most children have sunny dispositions if their home is happy and their needs are met. Other children seldom smile and little pleases them. You should be aware that you will naturally be drawn to the child who appears to have a love of life. You may also tend to spend less time with the child who appears sad, unhappy, or disagreeable most of the day. But regardless of this tendency, the child with a cloudy disposition needs your attention just as much as, and possibly more than, a child with a pleasant disposition.

In order to understand the child who exhibits a negative disposition, ask the following questions: (1) Does he show the same mood at home as he does away from home? (2) If so, has this been a characteristic of this child since birth? (3) If this is a recent characteristic or something that is portrayed only at home, what might be causing it? (4) What can I do to help this child overcome his moodiness? Has something in our home environment — such as a sick parent or watching television too late — caused his moodiness? Or might it be something outside the home, such as not having any friends at school?

A sudden change in the quality of moods a child has may give you a clue that all is not right, or it may be the first indication of illness. If you can find the cause, you can help your child in understanding his current situation or possibly in changing it.

Here are some of the things you can do to help a child overcome habitual moodiness:

1. Quit rewarding him for moodiness. Very often adults give a lot of time and attention to a child when he is down and out. Attention at this time is not good if it serves to reward and thus reinforce his moody behavior.

2. Look at your own behavior. Is it on days that you are moody that your child is also moody? Children are great reflectors of the adult image!

Even though a child may have from birth expressed a negative outlook on life, it is not impossible to change if you will consistently reward the child when he does break through with a smile. "I love to see you smile" may be all that needs to be said. But it is equally important not to draw too much attention to the negative — this is better left ignored.

Children sometimes pout to punish the rest of the family. The longer they stay alone in their rooms, the more control they exhibit over the family.

Every child deserves some time alone, but don't allow long periods of pouting. After five minutes or so, walk into your child's room; act as if you don't even realize he's pouting. Busy yourself with some task close to him. Talk to him, but don't expect an answer. You might rub his back, but if he resists don't act as if you've noticed. It's awfully hard to keep pouting when it has no effect!

Later, when it's all over, you can talk about how problems can be solved without pouting, so your child doesn't have to waste time feeling miserable!

Approach vs. Withdrawal

Some children easily approach new experiences, surroundings, or people, while others seem to almost turn tail and run. The child who has the "approach" characteristic is the curious one who learns by jumping in and often making mistakes, while the child with the "withdrawal" characteristic is the one who stands back and learns by the mistakes someone else makes. Both types of children have found their satisfying way of coping with new situations. However, it is sometimes necessary to teach approach-type children that in some situations it would be best to wait for instructions or permission, to make observations or just to think before plunging in. At the same time, the withdrawal-type children must be helped to feel safe enough so that they can approach people and tasks without a stifling fear of criticism or failure.

Consider the ages of the children. Between the ages of six and eight months, children tend to withdraw from strangers. This withdrawal may continue for two years or longer, so that the child continues to feel hesitant to step into new situations or go to strangers. What should parents do?

First of all, you can help your child feel comfortable and gain skills so that he will feel that he can safely approach people. But it won't happen overnight. During this six- to twelve-month period it must be a gradual process. Take it in little tiny steps; introducing the child first to close relatives or friends in the security of your home. Then leave the child momentarily with them while you go to another room. Gradually increase the time you are away. In this way you can help your child understand that other people are safe to be with.

Mothers who force their children into unwelcome situations only reinforce their tendency to withdraw. The more you push, the tighter your child will hold on. Allow your child to be himself — love him just the way he is. Then, eventually, he will realize that he can safely let go.

Don't just suddenly disappear, especially for long periods of time. This makes the child feel insecure and his tendency is to not allow you out of his sight. If you must leave, make sure the child is with someone familiar — and hopefully in a familiar place. If the child is old enough, explain you must go and when you'll be back and then matter-of-factly leave. Stay away long enough so a babysitter will have time to establish some rapport. Then come back on time.

Even though the withdrawal characteristic is something that is quite evident early in a child's life, nearly all children have periods in their growing up when they display shyness in social relationships. When parents understand this, they should not become unduly concerned when they see their child withdraw from people and materials when they first come into a preschool or school program. Watch to see if this is a temporary reaction to a new situation or if it becomes an habitual pattern.

The approach-type child is often called the impulsive child, and even though it may be disturbing for you to see a child constantly jumping into things without thinking, at least that child will learn by his mistakes. The child who needs more help is the shy, hesitant child.

It often makes a parent uncomfortable to see a shy child sitting or playing alone. Yet it is unfair for the adults to be always arranging thing so that the shy child never has to take the initiative to play with someone or something. When this happens — the shy child never has an opportunity to trust his own abilities to approach new situations.

This is not to say that parents should never try to make it easier for the shy child to approach activities or people, but only to caution not to get trapped into a habit. If parents make it easier once in a while, the shy children can learn that doing things with others can be fun and rewarding in themselves, as well as pleasing to their parent.

Persistence vs. Distractibility

Some children can concentrate on a task so completely that they seem oblivious to everything going on around them. They may not even hear you talking to them. Other children are distracted by the smallest interruption. In order to facilitate learning and concentration for the highly distractible child, it is important that you arrange the room in such a way that quiet activities, such as puzzles and games that need a high degree of attention in order to complete, are separated from more noisy activities. The feeling of success from completing a task is important for all children. But this is very difficult for the highly distractible. Just having the parent close or sitting beside this type of child can help him focus on the task. You should also do as much as you possibly can to limit outside distractions. For example, turn off the T.V. or stop talking on the phone when a child is trying to concentrate.

It is never possible to eliminate all of the distractions that come to a person; therefore, you should help a child learn to be persistent enough to finish a task even though there may be certain interruptions. This is a very important characteristic in order for children to solve problems and complete difficult projects. If a child enjoys a task and gets a feeling of accomplishment when it is finished, he will gradually learn to resist distraction in order to complete the task. You can help children develop persistence in the following ways:

1. Plan the daily schedule to allow enough time for your child to finish an activity without undue stress.

2. Plan projects that can be finished in a short time — usually not longer than one day.

3. Give your child a reason or an incentive to complete a project or task. For example: "It will be a surprise for Grandma." "That will look lovely on our wall." "You will feel good when you have finished this." "You may show Daddy what you have made."

4. Point out to your child the activity that will follow as soon as he finishes his task. For example: "You need to finish because we will be going to town soon, and we will need to put the materials away."

5. Give him encouragement. For example: "I will help

you if you need me." "It is almost completed." "Just one more piece."

6. Tell him you understand how he feels. For example: "I know it is hard, but I can help you." "I know you don't want to do it, but it will make your daddy happy." "I know it takes a long time, but you are almost finished." "I know you don't like to clean up, but it is time to go shopping." "You must have worked hard to get so much done."

7. You may have to point out to your child that "some things we do, not because we want to, but because it is good for us, or because we have to do them. It is good for you to learn to finish what you start."

8. Make a game out of finishing the task. For example: "It will surprise us to see what it is when it is finished." "What will it look like when it's finished?"

9. Reward him when he does finish. For example: "You look as if you are happy with what you have done." "It makes me happy when you finish what you begin." "Let's put it on the bulletin board."

10. Help him to find success with simple materials first. Substitute materials when a child is becoming frustrated because what he is working on is too difficult.

11. Do not pressure him into finishing every single task. It is important that he learns to finish tasks because it is meaningful and rewarding for him — not just to please you.

A little help at the right time, may boost the child over a discouraging difficulty and the satisfaction he will derive from seeing the task he undertook completed, will stimulate him to greater exertion. When it comes to persistence, here is a motto worth memorizing.

"One thing at a time, and that done well,

Is a very good thing, as all may tell.

Work with your will and all your might;

Things done by half are never done right."

Creativity vs. Conformity

Every child is unique. A child expresses his uniqueness through creativity and innovative behavior. When children do things in unusual ways or make something that no one else has made or find different solutions to a problem their parent thought had only one answer, then these children are being creative.

Creativity can be expressed in almost everything a child does — his words, songs, actions, art work and thinking. The creative child is not the easiest child to work with. Most parents will admit that they like the conformist, who always does things the expected way, and usually doesn't question what is asked of him. But it is the creative child who will ultimately contribute to new scientific discoveries or who will produce something that will bring enjoyment to many.

By the time a child reaches the preschool years some of the experiences in life may have already taught him that it is safer not to be too different — too creative. But whatever the age, children can be helped to develop creativity. Here are some of the things you can do to encourage creativeness:

1. Provide enough time and material for children to be creative. It is usually quicker and easier for a child to copy something someone else has made than to think of an original way of making something himself. To be creative takes time, and material must be available.

2. Accept creative behavior. You, as a parent, must be convinced that individuality is important and that not every child needs to act in the same way.

3. Create an atmosphere which encourages your children to be creative. Children should be made to feel

free to use materials in a variety of ways. For example, the blocks can be used to trace various shapes on paper as well as for building. In order to feel this free with materials your children should know the location of supplies he is free to use and should be encouraged to experiment in different ways.

4. Make comments and ask questions to stimulate creativity. For example: "There are many ways to put the paint on the paper." "How many different ways can you put on the paint?" "How many different things can you use this object for?" "That's interesting — I never thought about doing it that way."

5. Reward creative behavior in such a way that your child will have an intrinsic feeling of worth. For example: "That's a good idea." "You thought of a new way of doing this." "You look as if you enjoyed making this picture."

6. Do not make models in activities where your children can be self-expressive. For example, make a rhythm activity "creative movement" not "imitative movement." Do NOT say, "A duck walks like this." But say, "How many different ways can you walk like a duck?" "You be your own duck — this is the way I do it sometimes." "How do you feel like doing it?"

Do NOT say, "This is walking music." But say, "How many different ways can you walk?" (Backward, sideways, high, low, fast, slow, on tiptoes, on heels, etc.)

In art work do NOT say, "What colors should a tree be?" or "The tree should be green." But say, "You have made a tree that no other person has made. It is your very own. I really like your tree."

7. Provide opportunities for your child to make up stories, poems and songs. Sometimes after a child has painted a picture, you can ask him to tell a story about his picture.

8. Be creative yourself. Don't do the same thing over

and over again, but try something new. In every activity there is room for creativity. Not everything will work, but your child will learn that whether it works or not, you have the courage to try something different.

To give one idea of how you can be creative with music, make music from materials that are not usually thought of as musical instruments. For example: gourds can be shaken; nails hanging from strings can be hit together; different sizes of pipes can be hit with a mallet; wood doweling can be hit together; blocks covered with sandpaper can be scraped together; jingle bells put on strings of elastic can be put over a child's arms and legs and can be jingled to rhythm; coconut halves can be hit together; clothespins clipped to a piece of cardboard make an interesting sound when a mallet is run across them; large tin cans with innertube rubber over the ends can be used as drums; even half-filled jars of water hit with a spoon can make music. The possibilities are endless.

9. Create an atmosphere where mistakes and failures are accepted as a part of the creative experience. It has been said that when you are creative, there is no such thing as making a mistake. How many times did Thomas Edison try over and over to make something work? Was he successful? Many children are not pleased with the outcome when they try something one way and find that their product does not have the effect that they wanted. For example, a child may mix two colors and not get the color he wanted; or he may try to balance blocks in a certain way, and it doesn't work. People who are inventive and creative often have more failures than successes! But the secret of success is that they are able to accept their failures and are eager to try again.

Generosity vs. Selfishness

It is typical of a very young child to think that the world revolves around himself, that he is the most important person in the world, and that everyone should cater to his needs. When a child has this feeling, it is difficult, or almost impossible, for him to think about anything but getting what he wants. Slowly, as your child has his needs met by you so that he feels secure and happy, he should learn to reach out to help or to share with others.

Sharing or waiting for turns is very difficult for the two-year-old child. There may be fewer conflicts at this age if you have a number of the same kind of toys when another child of the same age comes to play. By four years of age when imagination and sensitivity to others is beginning to develop, it becomes much easier for a child to share. It is at about eight years of age that we find generosity at its peak. Then a child will give away your most desired possessions if you don't watch him. The generous person is willing to adjust his own needs and desires to the needs and desires of others. In helping a child learn to share, you should remember the following points:

1. Do not force a child to share. It is possible to make children share, but the act of sharing without the feeling of sharing does not obtain the desired effect of making a child more willing to share the next time. For example, Alice may give up her favorite doll but is angry about having to do it and determines that next time she will hide it so she won't have to share.

It is also true that some children, even at four or five years of age, still have a strong attachment to their own things. If a child brings something of his own to your home, he should not have to share that item. However, that child may have to accept the consequence of you putting his toy away if your children are too demanding over not being able to use it. Sometimes a child is unwilling to share because he is afraid someone else will damage his possessions. You can help by setting up a situation where it will be kept safe and then reassuring the child that you will supervise the situation so that nothing will happen to his possession.

In a situation where there is only one toy and a child has been waiting for a very long time for his turn, it may be necessary to set some time limitations upon the use of the toy by any one person. Warning a child that he has five more minutes may make it easier for him to give up the toy rather than just arbitrarily coming up and taking the toy away and giving it to another child.

2. Help your children to handle sharing situations by themselves. It is always better if children can be taught to share on their own without having you force your way on them. When a child wants something another child has, have him say to the other child, "When you are finished, may I have it, please?" At first the other child may say, "No." It is then your job to explain to the child that when he is finished he won't want it anymore. When the child is finally finished, he may forget to tell the child who wanted the toy that he is finished, and you must remind him to tell the first child that it is now his turn. In this way the child who was initially unwilling to share, experiences the pleasure from having shared as he sees how happy he has made the other child.

3. Generosity does not usually come spontaneously; it is learned. You must continually encourage and reward a generous and sharing attitude among your children. You must make it attractive for them to share.

The specific characteristics mentioned in this chapter are only a few of the ways in which children are unique. Understanding these characteristics and the different ways that parents can work with children either to stimulate or to modify their behavior should be helpful to you as you seek to understand your children better.

Understanding Emotions

Parents often find that dealing with a child's emotions and the behavior caused by those emotions is one of the most difficult and perplexing tasks with which they have to cope. The reason for this is that when a child is emotionally upset, his body is in such a state that reasoning with him is ineffectual. In many cases this frustrates the adult to such a degree that his own emotions begin to be aroused.

An emotion has been defined as a stirred-up state of the body. When a person is experiencing an emotion, there are certain changes in the person's feelings and his observable behavior, such as laughing, crying, fighting, frowning, being "silly" or being moody. But more than these superficial effects, emotions also produce changes in certain bodily functions, such as blood circulation, breathing, gland activity and sensory processes.

In order to understand better the changes that take place during an emotional reaction, let's "observe" Danny, a typical three-year-old child who has been sitting on the floor of a babysitter's home for almost half an hour building a complicated, tall, intricately balanced block structure. He is comfortable and happy, thinking about how pleased his mother will be when she comes to pick him up in a few minutes. His heart is beating normally. His stomach is digesting the food he has eaten for lunch. His lungs are supplying only the necessary amount of oxygen, while his liver is storing minute amounts of blood sugar. Suddenly Tom, a big impulsive five-year-old, runs across the room and kicks down Danny's entire building.

Danny is startled — his large muscles give an involuntary jerk as the blocks crash to the floor. He drops the block he was holding in his hand and gives a small shriek. Adrenalin flows into his bloodstream, and this in turn causes the liver to release its supply of blood sugar, giving Danny an energy boost. His heart quickens its beat as blood pounds through his temples. The digestive actions cease in his stomach. His mouth starts to dry. His hair follicles tighten. The pupils of his eyes dilate. His nostrils expand to accommodate the increased oxygen required by his lungs. Beads of sweat break out on his forehead. His first impulse is to hit Tom. But he can't think clearly about how to place the blow, and he is uncertain about the consequences.

Just as Danny is starting to cry, his mother appears and puts a comforting arm around him. He feels weak all over and falls into his mother's arms sobbing deeply and shaking unsteadily. In a few minutes he has recovered his composure enough to tell his mother what has happened. He then feels relaxed. Before leaving, Danny stops at the restroom and then falls asleep in the car on his way home.

During a strong emotion, the heart beats faster, the stomach stops digesting, the saliva stops flowing, the blood vessels become constricted and perspiration increases. This is the function of the sympathetic division of the autonomic nervous system which dominates during an emotion. Just following the emotional reaction, the parasympathetic division dominates, causing the heart to slow down, the stomach to start digesting and the saliva to flow. Then, after a short time, balance is restored.

When you realize how emotions cause a child's — or an adult's — body functions to be thrown out of balance, you can understand why it is important to avoid situations that might arouse strong negative emotions. You must first learn to control your own emotional reactions, because the expression of strong emotions tends only to arouse the same response in others. You should also be aware that when children are displaying strong emotions, it is likely that you will experience an emotionalized response. This only complicates the situation further, leading to greater misunderstandings and often to harsh discipline in order to control the emotionally aroused child.

Children learn, especially in the area of emotions, by watching their parents, other significant adults or even older children. When children see others express emotions of frustration and anger in harsh and unreasonable ways, they learn that such action is appropriate and they copy it. It is good counsel to not let harsh or angry words escape your lips. You cannot with safety be emotionally overbearing, demeaning and out-of-control. Your words and the tone in which they are spoken are lessons to your children on how to handle emotions!

Of course, we all make mistakes and occasionally lose control, but we should remember that, "Ideals are like stars. We may never reach them, but we can set our course by them." And setting a right course in the area of your own emotional behavior will prove doubly beneficial since it will be reflected in the lives of your children.

When parents understand how strong emotions affect not only a child's observable behavior but also his body functions, they will be more understanding in their expectations for the child. For example, when your child is emotionally upset, it is extremely difficult for him to eat, sleep or even learn. These activities must wait until he is over his emotional reaction and his body is back in balance.

There are many emotions. The more positive ones promote family health and personal happiness: affection, delight, elation, excitement, hope and joy. Those with negative components, however, are troublesome: anger, anxiety, disgust, distress, disappointment, envy, fear, jealousy and shame. It is important that you learn something about these emotions and what causes them in children in order to be more effective in dealing with them when they do occur. Following are some of the most common emotions with which parents must cope.

Anger

Anger is the most common negative emotion in infancy and early childhood. A child must early be taught to cope with and to control his angry feelings, since these feelings can cause him to lose control over his actions. Helping your child make this conquest is an important challenge.

Children express anger in many ways. Usually for younger children anger is expressed in temper tantrums, screaming, holding his breath, or aggressive acts such as hitting and biting. As children become older, they often learn that they get punished when they express anger openly; so they try to express anger in other ways, such as pouting, planning revenge, thumbsucking, excessive eating, withdrawal and silence.

Children become angry over many things. A very common cause for younger children is parental interruption of their interesting activities (such as pouring water on the floor). Anger is frequently the result when a parent tries to get a child to do something that he doesn't want to do (such as getting dressed or sitting on the toilet).

A child's angry behavior changes as he gets older. During the first three years, most of a child's angry outbursts are undirected energy released in hitting, biting or some other use of the body. These outbursts come suddenly and many times without much warning. They may happen frequently, but they are usually over in less than five minutes. As children get older, anger becomes more directed toward the object or person that brought on the anger; it is less violent, more symbolic, and more verbal.

As children begin to associate with other children, there is an increase in angry outbursts because of conflicts over playthings; there are sometimes physical attacks between children or name-calling. Children also become angry when they are unable, with their limited vocabulary, to make others understand what they are saying or what they want.

It is not simple or easy to understand or deal with anger. Very often a child becomes upset easily if he is not feeling well, even though it may be only a slight illness, such as constipation or a cold. Anger is more common among children who are recovering from a serious illness than it is among children who have not been ill. It also seems that more outbursts in children occur before mealtimes than at any other time of the day. The reason for this is probably twofold. The children are tired and irritable because of low blood sugar, and parents are usually busier at this time making meal preparations and are not able to supervise their children as closely or meet their emotional needs for love and attention.

Anger is also related to the child's environment. The more adults (bosses giving conflicting orders) there are in the home, for example, the more likely a child is to have outbursts of anger. When parents shift from one method of control to another, there are more outbursts. It has also been found that children who were being toilet-trained showed more outbursts on days following bed-wetting than on days following dry nights. Apparently they are disappointed with their behavior and become frustrated. It has also been found that conflicts and outbursts are more frequent among nursery school children in a small play area than in a larger space. Limited toys and the others interfering with what one child wants to do leads to problems. This is why the back seat of small family cars is so often the scene of sibling battles.

One of the reasons why the expression of anger is so common in young children is that it does not take a child long to discover that the use of anger is a quick and easy way to get what he wants. Parents do not like to see their child angry. Therefore, without thinking, they begin reinforcing his angry behavior by giving him what he wants in order to pacify him, rather than waiting until he is over his emotional outburst.

During the preschool years boys tend to have more angry outbursts than do girls, possibly because parents are usually less disapproving of temper outbursts in boys than in girls.

In general, when a child is allowed to become frustrated, no matter what the cause, you can expect some type of expression of anger and be ready to help him deal with his anger in constructive ways rather than destructive, hurtful ways. Your child's feelings of anger should not be denied, for feelings are very real to children. Your child should not be made to feel guilty because he has these feelings; he should be taught to cope with them constructively.

One way he can learn is through your behavior. You may become angry over certain things, but you don't have to act out your angry feelings. Even though angry, you can still behave in a calm, unemotional way and use these feelings to change the situation that caused the anger in the first place. Because anger can be caused by so many different things, it is important for you to determine the causes and treat these, rather than just reacting to the anger itself.

Don't feel threatened when your child becomes angry. Remember, he is an unsocialized child and may be acting normally (even though undesirably) for his age. You, on the other hand, are an adult and with mature self-control can weather your child's emotional storms.

Here are some suggestions that may help to prevent children from becoming angry or showing their anger in undesirable ways.

1. Self-control in you is likely to be the best guarantee of self-control in your child.

2. Your child should not have too many bosses giving conflicting instructions and having conflicting expectations. Parental cooperation is of utmost importance.

3. Each child should have consistent discipline and guidance given at the first signs of frustration rather than waiting until he is forced to express his anger in a hurtful or destructive manner.

4. Your child should be cared for on a flexible routine which provides food, rest and activity before he is acutely and painfully in need of these things.

5. Efforts should be made to avoid over-excitement and over-fatigue.

6. You should answer a child's calls for help promptly, before he becomes frustrated.

7. You should not permit your child to get what he wants by angry outbursts; i.e., do not reinforce anger.

8. Help your child learn how to get what he wants through unemotional behavior. This may mean teaching him to ask for something, to wait his turn, to reason or persuade, or even to say "please."

9. Calmly help your child find satisfactory substitutes for things he wants but can't have, before he becomes frustrated.

10. An atmosphere of emotional warmth should pervade your home. When a child's life is filled with positive emotions there is less chance that negative emotions will be expressed.

11. Express clearly what behavior is permitted and what is not. For example, "You may not scream at me. When you talk in a soft voice I will listen."

Aggression

Aggressive behavior, such as appropriate self-assertiveness, is an important attribute for all children to acquire; but when aggressive behavior is accompanied by anger, the sparks fly, and this leads only to more difficulty. Aggressiveness in this sense means attack, intrusion, provocation, being pushy or committing the first act which leads to a quarrel or an attack.

Aggressiveness is one form an angry outburst can take, and it is one of the hardest forms of negative emotional behavior that parents must deal with. The causes for aggression are similar to the causes for anger. For example, aggression may be a reaction to frustration, or may be related to physical factors such as hunger and fatigue, but it may also be causd by a desire for attention or to demonstrate superiority.

Aggression may also come from feelings of insecurity which make a child feel that he needs to be on the defensive as a means of self-protection. "If I act first, I will be in control of the situation."

Very often a child becomes physically aggressive when he is not able to express himself. He may want to enter a play group or want something someone else has, but because of his poor verbal skills he can't make anyone understand him. Usually, as children learn to communicate verbally, their need to hit other children decreases. Much of the inter-child aggression occurs between children of two different ages, with the younger the less aggressive. Some of this aggression seems to be caused by the older child's lack of ability to get the younger child to understand his words.

How a child's peers react to his aggressive behavior has a lot to do with either increasing or decreasing his aggressive acts. For example, if a younger child cries when he's hit by an angry sibling, the crying rewards the child who hit. It accomplished what he wanted and he learns that hitting is effective. But if the child who is hit shows no reaction, then the child isn't rewarded for hitting and the frequency of hitting as a way to solve a problem is usually decreased.

Aggressive behavior is very easily modeled. Children often ignore what adults or parents say ("Don't hit!") and continue to do what adults do (hit). For example, when Bonnie became angry at school, she would pick up the nearest item and throw it. When the teacher brought this to the mother's attention, the mother explained that Bonnie's behavior sounded just like her husband's actions when he was angry. It has been demonstrated conclusively that children learn aggressive behavior from viewing violent motion pictures or cartoons. They even enlarge upon the model, inventing more aggressive actions.[5]

Parents often have difficulty knowing when an aggressive act is just part of a child's self-assertion and when it may be harmful. In general, a child's aggression becomes harmful when (1) it exceeds the demands of the situation, (2) it is so intense that it breaks out in destructive acts, (3) it is directed against people with an intent to injure them rather than against things and conditions that should be changed, (4) it is turned inward and arouses strong feelings of guilt and anxiety in the child.

It is always better if we can prevent our children from becoming harmfully aggressive. How?

1. By reducing frustrations and avoiding conditions

that are provoking, especially when your child is too immature to control his intense feelings. This takes a lot of good observation and prompt action.

2. By being aware of children who have a low tolerance for frustration and are oversensitive, excitable and quick to show wrath.

3. By recognizing your child's feelings — recognizing when he begins to be angry — and working with the problem immediately.

4. By talking about your child's feelings, being open, letting it be allowable to verbalize anger.

5. By helping to direct aggressive impulses into constructive work or active play or symbolic behavior like painting or imaginative playacting.

6. By helping to release tension so that feelings are not bottled up only to be released in an even larger explosion.

Children must be helped to see that feelings of anger and aggression will naturally arise. It is what a person does with those feelings that is important. It is a child's actions that count; and slowly, with your calm guidance, the child can learn to put strong emotional feelings to good constructive use. When children are taught to bring these feelings out into the open immediately as they arise and deal constructively with them, they learn not to harbor resentment, anger, or hate. You must be tolerant of these feelings and make it safe for your child to express them, while at the same time not accepting the harmful aggression that may be a result of these feelings.

Especially in dealing with aggression, you must firmly state the limitations to your child, "You may not harm yourself, others, or things" and reinforce these limitations in a *nonaggressive way*. Spanking can be considered aggressive behavior and is too often done in anger. Therefore, using spanking as a method of correcting a child's aggression is usually not as effective as using parent-imposed logical consequences and behavior modification techniques such as time-out periods. Parents who have children who express little aggression, strongly disapprove of hostile aggression and stop it firmly without using physical or aggressive punishment.

Temper Tantrums

Temper tantrums are another way a young, preschool child may express anger at conditions that he can't handle. A tantrum may take the form of violent behavior such as kicking, biting, and pounding his head against the floor, or it may take the form of destructiveness, attempted injury of others, or verbally ridiculing and criticizing others.

Temper tantrums usually begin between one and two years of age. After about two and one-half years, the outbursts in connection with the establishment of routines tend to decrease, while conflicts with authority and frustration in social situations tend to increase. An occasional temper tantrum between two and three years of age can be expected for most children but must be handled in such a way that they will not be likely to continue throwing one when angry again.

When a girl five years old (or older) has frequent temper tantrums, they may be associated with other disturbing behavior, such as irritability, overdependence, insufficient appetite, somberness, negativism, attention-demanding and fear. When this is the case, it may be wise to consult the child's pediatrician, or even a child psychiatrist, in order to overcome the child's disturbed state.

Temper tantrums in boys five years old (or older) are associated with negativism, but not necessarily the general disturbed state that is characteristic of girls.

Searching for a reason for this difference between girls and boys, we may find that we are more lenient with boys and allow them to act out more of their emotions. But with girls the free expressions of anger and hostile aggression are not as acceptable. Therefore, their tantrums very often indicate more than just negativism.

How a parent handles a temper tantrum has a lot to do with whether or not it will recur. If the tantrum is successful in getting what the child wants, the child soon learns that throwing a tantrum is effective and tantrums can become habitual.

Most tantrums are thrown to get the adult's attention so that the child can influence the adult to give him his own way. When the parent walks away and ignores the unacceptable behavior, the child ceases to have a reason for throwing the tantrum. That's why ignoring is so effective in stopping tantrums. In doing this it is important for you to make sure your child or other children around him will not get hurt or that objects will not be damaged. It may also be disturbing for other children to see your child behaving in this unacceptable way while you "ignore" it. If this is the case, you should simply explain, "John wants to ride a bike and he thinks that if he acts this way I will get one for him. He must learn that yelling and crying are not the ways to ask for help. When he is finished acting this way, I will help him."

It is impossible to talk to or reason with a child during a tantrum, and it is not a good idea to try, since it is rewarding to get so much attention while acting in such an unacceptable way. As soon as your child has obtained control over his emotional behavior, you can talk to him. At this time you should make your child understand clearly that this type of behavior is not allowed. He will not get what he wants when he acts this way.

Then, to help your child learn appropriate ways to

behave when he is upset, you can suggest the following: "I will listen to you and try to help you when you ask me kindly. If I'm busy and not paying attention, pull on my coat and tell me you are getting angry so I will know it is very important that I listen. I will try to help you so you won't have to get angry and act this way, because when you do, you will not get what you want and that makes you unhappy."

If temper tantrums persist it is important to find the reason. It may be that this is the way your child behaves at the babysitters. If so, work together in solving this problem. *Try to alleviate the cause.* If it always happens when he is tired, try not to let him get too tired. If it is when he is hungry, keep a close eye on him before mealtimes to stop the behavior before it builds up.

Remember that bad habits, which temper tantrums can become, are always harder to break after they have become established.

Here are some suggestions to stop tantrums.

1. Don't reward your child by giving him what he wants. If he wants attention, walk away. If he wants a toy or some other thing, say, "No," and be firm!

2. When babies and small children lose control, you might hold them in your arms, firmly yet gently. You might even sing a hymn during this time. Your control and calm strength may help them bring themselves under control.

3. Surprising children by your behavior sometimes proves successful. Parents have testified that many divergent and somewhat bizarre parental behavior has stopped temper tantrums, such as a cold shower, watching the tantrums but showing no expression at all, throwing a tantrum beside the child or totally ignoring the child, even though you are in the same room. It's as if the child says, "I quess I'd better not throw another

tantrum, because I don't know what Mom or Dad might do next!"

Remember, you may ignore a temper tantrum, but don't be indifferent to it. After it is over and your child is in control, talk to him about his inappropriate behavior and give him ways he can cope in the future without losing control.

Quarreling

Quarreling is another expression of anger. It is common in a young child's interactions. Someone has suggested that even though the average childish quarrel lasts less than thirty seconds, it happens about every five minutes in a group of preschoolers. Quarreling is a normal result of a child's social interaction. Those children who have more social contacts have more quarrels. It is also true that friends quarrel more than nonfriends. Children at this age are naturally egocentric (they think the world revolves around them) and are often unable to put themselves in the place of others. This way of thinking naturally causes conflicts with anyone who may hold differing opinions. If the other person is also egocentric in his thinking, a quarrel is very likely to occur.

Most quarrels need no adult intervention; they are the child's way of finding where he stands and expressing his opposing opinion. Quarrels become harmful when things are said in anger that are meant to hurt the other person. It is then that you must guide your children to a more kind and acceptable way of interacting.

Some of the following questions and comments may help children to change their quarreling behavior: "How does it make you feel when John calls you dummy?" "It makes me sad when I hear children saying mean things to each other." "I wouldn't like it if someone said that to me." "What did you want Mary to do that made you so angry?" "Let's think of a kind way of trying to get Mary to help you." Be careful when asking, "How would you feel?" to a child who has said something hurtful. A preschooler will very often say, "I would feel good!"

Time-out is an appropriate way to handle excessive or hurtful quarreling. (See Chapter 4 under "Techniques of Discipline.")

Children learn relational skills by the experience of interacting with other children. It may not be fun for adults to listen to their social blunders and quarreling, but it is important for children to have these experiences as they progress to more socially acceptable and mature ways of relating.

Jealousy and Rivalry

Jealousy is a combination of the feelings of anger and fear — anger because a child is frustrated in his desire to be loved best; and fear because of possibly losing the love of his parents, teacher or another meaningful person. Rivalry is the angry feeling that comes when a child becomes frustrated in his desire or attempt to do the best or to win. Jealousy and rivalry can both be detrimental to a child's healthy personality development.

Among preschool children, jealousy is usually aroused when either the parents or a primary caregiver seem to shift their interest and attention to someone else. Jealousy can be aroused when a parent babysits another child and must devote a lot of time helping this new child feel comfortable. Your child who is used to having all of your attention suddenly feels that you don't love him as much because you don't spend as much time with him. During this adjustment period the older children in the family can be encouraged to help the new child feel comfortable while you make sure you spend as much time as possible with the child feeling jealous. When you need to be with the new child, you might find that children of three or four years of age can begin to understand the situation if you speak frankly to them and say, "John feels very bad right now because he misses his mother, so he needs me to hold him." "Sometimes when you get hurt or feel bad you need me to hold you, but now it is John's time." It may also be helpful if you warned your children that a new child will be coming to your home because he needs someone to care for him, and discuss the possibility of jealous feelings and how these can be handled before the child arrives.

Within families, it is interesting to note that the firstborn is more likely to be jealous than younger children. Jealousy within the family tends to decrease as the family size increases. There is also more jealousy in homes in which the parents are oversolicitous, inconsistent or poorly adjusted.

Young children's jealousy is usually directed against another person — the individual who the child believes has usurped his place in the loved one's affections. Jealousy sometimes causes the child to revert to old habits or immature behaviors, such as thumb-sucking, bed-wetting, general naughtiness, bidding for attention by refusing to eat, or by pretending to be ill or afraid.

Jealousy usually begins when a new baby is born into the family and the older child feels his parents love the baby more. Why? Because parents spend so much time with the baby. In the child's mind, attention (time) and love are equated. The more attention the parents give to another, the more the child feels they love the other. Here are some suggestions:

1. Begin preparing your older child to receive the newborn well before the baby is born. It takes a young child time to get used to the idea that another child will be sharing his parent's attention.

2. Paint a realistic picture of how life will be with the baby. Don't say the baby will be a wonderful playmate, or say how much your child will love the baby. Neither may be true at birth! Say something like this, "God has created every child to have a special place within a family. And our family (Mommy, Daddy and Junior) is very blessed that God has chosen us to be the home of a special baby. Babies are special — but they are not always easy to live with. They can't talk, so they have to cry when they want something. They can't eat by themselves, so we will have to feed our baby. And they can't even go to the bathroom by themselves, so we will have to change his messy pants. Babies take a lot of time, so all three of us will have to work together to take care of the baby. And just when I sit down to read you a story, or start to help you build with your blocks, the baby may start crying to tell us he is hungry, or needs his pants changed. What do you think we should do?"

Having talked about specific situations that are likely to occur and having your child provide the answer that you should help the baby during this time, will help him better accept the situation when it actually happens.

3. Encourage your child to feel that the baby belongs to the whole family and not just mom and dad.

4. Help your child prepare a gift for the newborn baby, just as the wisemen brought gifts to Baby Jesus. You may also want to get a gift for the baby to give to your older child.

5. Some parents have purchased a special doll for their child that is given to him when the baby comes home. Then as mommy takes care of the real baby, the child can take care of the doll.

6. Talk about how each person can contribute to the others in the family. Mention things that your child can do for the baby, and also, what the baby can do for your child; for example, warm your child's bed before he gets

into it, make your child laugh, hold your child's finger, etc.

7. As soon as possible after the baby is born, let your child see, touch and hold the baby so he feels he is not being kept from the baby.

8. When the baby comes home, don't force your older child to be with you when you must be in intimate contact with the baby, such as when you are breast feeding or bathing the baby. Seeing mommy and baby together often engenders feelings of jealousy, especially when mom doesn't have an extra arm or lap to hold the older child. It may be helpful to have others contribute to the care of the baby for the first few days, so mom can have extra time and two free hands to reassure the older child of her love.

9. Be prepared to pass the love-test. Love-testing is something that very often occurs when a new baby joins the family. The child sees mom and dad spending so much time with the baby that he begins to feel they love the baby more than him, so he tests their love by doing something forbidden, like waking the sleeping baby or dumping over the diaper pail. If you scream at your child and punish, you will fail the love-test, because your child will feel that you do love the baby more. But the child cannot be satisfied with this answer so he continues to test. The only way to nip this testing behavior is to convince your child at the first love-test that he is loved supremely, not more or less, but as much as you can possibly love. Try this when the test occurs: "I bet you think I love the baby more than you because I have had to spend so much time with the baby and that is why you.... (tore up the baby book), but you are wrong. I love you very, very much." Then ignore the misbehavior and spend some pleasant time together. After a while you might say, "When you begin to feel like your love cup is empty and that I love the baby more, just come over

to me and tell me your love cup is empty and I'll fill you up to overflowing!''

Let me warn you, passing the love-test does not come naturally. Every nerve in your body will feel like punishing. But if you do, chances are the love-testing will continue!

10. As your older child accepts the baby and wants to help with its care, don't discourage him just because you can do things more efficiently. Look for little, helpful things your child can do and give him credit for his efforts. Reward the motive of wanting to help — even though the opposite may occur at times.

Rivalry among children, although common, is not necessarily healthy. It can lead to excessive competition, lying, cheating and selfishness. And it can create misery and chaos in the home.

Rivalry can be caused by many things, such as allowing one child to boss others, showing favoritism, permitting competitions or even creating boredom through not providing enough different things to do. In order to prevent as much rivalry as possible, try the following:

1. Make sure you spend some time daily with each child to give that child a feeling of being special. If one child is a particularly demanding child, and it seems difficult to show "equal" time, it might be wise to plan time together on a weekly basis, so each child can look forward to time when he or she can be alone with you.

2. Look for something positive to say about each child. Be observant enough to notice little things like the combed hair, tied shoe laces or the "please" that was said without prompting. Be careful that your words of appreciation do not make your other children feel guilty for not having done the same thing. Each child should receive enough positive recognition to feel satisfied and confident of his parent's admiration.

3. Avoid comparisons between children. Since all

children like to be the best or the fastest or the cleanest, parents often fall into the trap of using comparisons between children in order to motivate them to do their best or to conform to what the parent requires. If you say, "Look how Linda cleaned up her plate. Who is going to have a clean plate next?" this comment may get your children to eat all of their food, but it also fosters rivalry among them since it places Linda as the best "cleaner-upper" in the family.

It is sometimes difficult to avoid comparisons among your children. For example, your two children have been playing with blocks. Larry has built a fantastic structure that is almost as high as he is, completely symmetrical, and balanced delicately, while Joe has succeeded in stacking only a few blocks. You feel you should make some comment. What should you say?

The most typical reaction would be to say to Larry, "What a fantastic building," and say nothing to Joe. But in doing this, a very obvious comparison is made. Some parents say the same thing to each child. "What a nice building — I like it." But Joe knows that you really don't mean it, because it is obvious, even to him, that his is not as nice. *The secret is to be specific.* No comparisons are made when you say to Larry, "I like the way you have made the blocks balance," and then say to Joe, "I like your bridge; I think I can find a little car to go under it if you would like."

4. If children are interested in competition or "beating a record," let it be their own. It doesn't matter how talented someone else is, what matters is that your child is doing his best and is willing to develop the talent he has. You might tell your children the Bible story of the talents. (Matthew 25:14-30.) Everyone was given a different number of talents but what counted was what they did with what they had!

5. Focus on each child's uniqueness. Let your children know that God created them with differences

because He has a different work for each one of them to do. Even within the family they can play a different, but equally valuable role. Encourage each child to notice and to compliment each other on the special abilities and skills that they develop. Make every child feel like a superstar in some area that is different from his siblings. *Within the family* a superstar bedmaker can be as important as a superstar pianist, even though others outside the family may value things differently.

6. Treat all children fairly — but not in exactly the same manner. Even young children are aware of favoritism and will be quick to pick out "daddy's pet." It is possible for parents to be drawn to one child more than to another. You should be aware of this and, regardless of your feelings toward a child, treat all children fairly.

Physical appearance and intelligence, two characteristics over which your child has little control, are the two things that make a child initially attractive. People are naturally drawn to the cute child who learns quickly. When a parent is having difficulty accepting a child, it may even be helpful to spend more time with that child and do more with him. Very often feelings follow actions. The more time a parent spends with a child, the more attractive qualities he sees and appreciates.

It is impossible to treat all children in exactly the same manner, and it should not even be attempted. Since all children are different and unique, your interactions with each child should reflect this difference. Children do not want to be treated exactly alike. They want to be treated like the individuals they actually are.

7. Encourage your children to extend their friendships beyond their own siblings, cousins or special friends. When children associate only with their own close friends, it is common for them to gang up and treat an outsider as a rival. "You don't belong in our yard."

"You can't play with us!" When children are encouraged to make friends with new children, "outsiders" can become their friends and not their rivals.

Fear

Around six months of age almost all young children show fear of falling, of loud, sudden, unfamiliar noises, and of unfamiliar animals, faces or rooms. After one year of age children begin to be afraid of being alone and of being in the dark. During the preschool years (from approximately two and one-half to five years of age) certain fears normally decrease, such as fear of strangers and unfamiliar situations, sudden noise or movement, and falling or pain, while other fears increase. These include realistic fears such as traffic, drowning, fire or being alone and in the dark, as well as some unrealistic fears.

A group of seven, eight or nine-year-olds, asked what they fear most, will likely list such things as demons, ghosts, corpses or wild animals, such as bears, tigers and lions. Why should they fear those things? What are the chances of meeting any of them in the backyard? How do they develop these fears? Could it be that parents and older siblings say such things as, "The goblins will get you?" Or perhaps they see these things in a horror movie or TV show. To young children, seeing *is* believing — even if only on TV.

It doesn't matter to the young child whether the fear is real or imaginary, for, to the child, the feeling of fear is the same. Therefore, just telling your child, "You don't need to be afraid," or "There is nothing to be scared of," is not really very helpful, since it only disregards your child's genuine feeling of fear which he really is experiencing. *Fear arises according to the extent a child perceives himself as being unable to cope with a situation and therefore causes him to feel threatened.*

As children grow older and more experienced, many fears which were once displayed are replaced by feelings of confidence and reactions of pleasure. For example, the child who at two years of age fears to duck his head under water may three years later be jumping from a ten-foot high diving board. The two-year-old who feared dogs may have an inseparable shaggy pal at seven years of age.

Among older children, girls usually express their fears more readily than boys but this does not mean that boys are any less fearful. They have just been taught that it is not as acceptable for them to show they are afraid. If you realize this, you can help your child to understand that there is nothing weak or sissy about expressing a fear. Talking about fears and learning how others overcome their fears will help him to overcome his fear.

During the school-age years, fears of not being accepted or of failing become very important. Every child wants to be accepted as a part of the group. No child wants to be thought of as "different," and therefore, children may go to great effort to conform to the expectations of others. Every child wants to be successful in school, but many children feel they might fail. For example, quite a large percentage of children fear they may flunk the grade they are in, while in reality very few are asked to repeat a grade. Fears of not being accepted or of failing may not be very realistic, but you must realize that to children these fears are real.

Many fears arise at the time of a child's illness even though they may not be traced directly to the illness. Therefore, after a child has been sick and his regular routine disturbed, he may need more understanding and closeness.

The more perceptive a two-year-old is, the more fears he will probably possess, because he sees more dangerous situations than others and knows he doesn't have the capabilities to cope with them. But by the time children are five years old, this difference has usually disappeared; the intelligent child, although he may still perceive more fears, now is able to think of more effective ways of coping with them.

Fear is not always debilitating. It can save a child's life. In some situations it can lead to faster action, greater muscular exertion and more intensely concentrated effort than otherwise would be possible. But fear can lead also to panic, a disorganized and disruptive emotion which gets in the way of effective action, which paralyzes instead of stimulates and which breaks down even well-developed habits of efficient behavior. Therefore, children need to be taught to deal realistically with fear.

The following are some suggestions on how you can help your child to learn to cope with his fears:

1. Be an example. Although most children are naturally afraid of the sudden, unexpected happening such as a loud noise or falling, other fears are learned by being close to another fearful person. Very often a child's fears are very similar to his mother's fears. Children look to adults to learn how to behave in tense situations. For example, when a thunderstorm breaks, if you seem unconcerned, the children may relax. But if you show distress, the children may start crying or showing other fear responses.

It is important that your child learns, however, that you do have honest emotions, including fear, but have developed constructive ways to deal with these emotions.

2. Place a fearful child with other children who do not fear a certain situation. For example, if a child is afraid of a pet hamster, let him watch another child playing and having fun with the hamster. He can learn in this way to associate pleasant things with the pet, and this may give him courage to touch it and begin to learn that

his fears were unfounded and that he, too, can enjoy this experience.

3. Control the environment. Since a common factor in many fear situations is the suddenness and unexpectedness of the happening, whenever possible prepare a child by explaining what is going to happen. You can also try to control fear by not exposing children to objects or animals that may move suddenly. For example, for a very young child it may be better to introduce him to a worm, a kitten or a caterpillar, instead of a jumping frog, a snapping beetle, or even a jack-in-the-box.

4. Increase your child's adequacy for adjusting to difficult circumstances. A child's sense of fear is lessened when he is made to feel secure and he knows someone is looking out for his well-being. A parent's presence is very important to the fearful child. This feeling of closeness to an adult increases his adequacy in meeting new situations — "My mommy and I can handle it." It has also been found that the more a child is told about a potentially fearful situation, such as hospitalization, the less fearful he will be, since he will not only know what to expect but can begin to build his feelings of adequacy. Teach your child techniques for coping with situations where he feels inadequate. For example, in case he gets lost, he should know his parent's full name, address and telephone number.

5. Never force a child into a situation he fears. It is much better either to distract your child from the feared object or situation or to minimize the threat. For example, it may help to cage the animal which frightens him and then encourage him to approach it in such a way that no harm occurs to him. Throwing a child into the swimming pool does not cure his fear of water; patient teaching of swimming may.

6. Use your child's spontaneous expressions of fears which are displayed in his fantasy, dreams, dramatic

play or art work to gain insight into what he fears and why he does so.

7. Help your child to learn to associate pleasant things with the feared object or situation. Most fears are learned because children associate something threatening or painful with the feared object. Therefore, the most effective method of overcoming fear is to begin to associate a happy, satisfying experience with the object of fear. For example, if your child is afraid of policemen, you can arrange for a policeman to come to your home, where your child already feels comfortable and secure, rather than having him see a policeman in an unfamiliar situation. Arrange for the neighborhood children to meet the policeman when he drives up. When your child sees other children flock around the policeman, sit on his lap and perhaps ride on his shoulders, sit in his car, turn on the red light and talk over the radio, your child will begin to associate the policeman with a pleasant, enjoyable experience and may go closer to him and even talk with him. When this happens, his fear of policemen will slowly disappear.

8. Be open in talking about fear. Even though children's fears may be unrealistic, sometimes it is helpful just to talk about them, explaining why certain things are scary to children. Reading books about children's fears and about scary things often helps children open up and talk about things which they fear. Once these "fearful" things are discussed, they may seem less fearful.

When a child is afraid, it is good to reassure him that you are close and will protect him or will teach him how to protect himself. Recognize your child's fear; don't just disregard it. Say to him, "I know you are afraid, but I'm close to you." Say, "It's the thunder's job to make a loud noise," rather than saying, "Don't be afraid," or "You're not afraid of the thunder." Children need understanding, acceptance, and reassurance concerning their fears.

9. Help your child develop a sense of trust in adults and in God's protection. Be trustworthy. When you say you will do something, do it. If you promise your child you will return at a certain time, do it. As your child develops a trust in adults, it will be easier to trust in God.

Some children (and adults) experience extreme fear that can become a burden without the knowledge that God's presence is always with them. Bible stories of God's protection can help to instill this faith. Tell about Elisha in the mountain city when he saw a mighty host of angels between him and the enemy. Then there are the stories of how an angel delivered Peter from prison and how God protected Paul, the prisoner, and the others on the sinking ship. These stories were not written that we might read and merely wonder, but that the same faith which God's Bible servants had, might be in us. Help your child memorize the promise, "The angel of the Lord encampeth round about them that fear (love and respect) him, and delivereth them." Psalm 34:7. God can work in the same way in our lives today. We must be strong in faith and teach our children that we are all dependent upon God.

Children sometimes seem powerless to control intense irrational fears such as the fear of being kidnapped or of the house burning down. Sometimes these fears are exhibited in what is termed "night terrors," where children in a state of sleep scream hysterically and don't respond to their parent's comfort and reassurance. Testimonies of many parents confirm that in these situations there is power in prayer. Place your hands upon your child and in Jesus' name demand the spirit of fear to leave. God does not want a child's life plagued with irrational emotions and He does promise to help in seemingly helpless situations!

Signs of Possible Emotional Problems

It is important to understand and work with a child's

negative emotions in such a way that he doesn't feel guilty and inadequate. But parents should also be able to recognize when a child is suffering from problems that are deeper than an occasional emotional reaction to various situations. Deep, long-standing, emotional problems are complex and usually require not only the patience and insight of the parent, but in addition, the specialized therapy and counseling of a child psychologist or psychiatrist. Parents should be alert to signs of emotional distress and problems in children, for the earlier these problems are recognized the easier they can be resolved.

The following behaviors might indicate that all is not well with your child. Please note that none of these may be significant alone. But when they occur in combinations, you may have a key to a developing emotional problem.

1. Extreme nervousness or irritableness.

2. Inability to relax or rest.

3. Listlessness and/or excessive daydreaming.

4. Excessive inattention and tendency toward distraction.

5. Frequent unprovoked crying spells.

6. Lack of interest in surroundings or other children.

7. Unusual shyness and quietness.

8. Lack of laughter and smiles.

9. Overanxiousness about doing what is expected or "right."

10. Frequent hiding or attempting to run away.

11. Repeated aggression (both in words and in actions such as hitting or biting).

12. Destructiveness.

13. Frequent temper tantrums.

14. Frequent complaints of physical problems such as stomachaches or headaches.

15. Bed-wetting (after a period of dryness).

16. Unusual or unreasonable fears.

17. Marked personality and/or behavior changes.

18. Marked drop in grades (for child in school).

Why is it that some children display many wholesome emotions while others display negative ones? Emotional problems are often triggered by events and situations in a child's life that are particularly stressful. The following list indicates some of these potentially difficult periods.

1. Parental divorce.

2. Parental conflict in the home (family/child conflict as well).

3. Parental tension over work or personal problems.

4. Disruption of the home routine, such as too much company staying for too long a time.

5. New situations, like starting school or getting a new babysitter.

6. Dissatisfaction with one's own behavior, such as not being able to stay dry during the night.

7. Too much criticism of the child.

8. Unrealistic expectations of the child.

9. Lack of sufficient quality time together with the family.

10. Problems with making friends at school.

11. Scholastic pressures or difficulties (such as learning to read, meeting a deadline for an essay, etc.).

12. Illness, fatigue or the death of a family member.

Parental neglect may also be a factor causing the display of negative emotions in children. First, it may be that parents just do not give their children the attention and love they need to grow into healthy, secure individuals. Second, parents may neglect to correct and deal with negative emotions when they are first expressed and these emotions continue to grow into bad habits of behavior. Third, parents may neglect to provide an example of constructive ways to deal with negative emotions or fail to provide a continual expression of the positive emotions of happiness, joy, hope and affection.

In summary, children must learn that it is not wrong to experience negative feelings, but in dealing with these emotions they must act in a constructive way. In addition, parents have a responsibility to provide children with an emotionally "safe" environment and an example of cheerful living, for it is through the cultivation of positive emotions that beautiful characters are developed. Paul gave excellent advice when he said that we should concentrate on things that are noble, just, pure, lovely and of good report — and rejoice in the Lord always. (Philippians 4:8 and 4).

. . . whosoever heeds correction gains understanding. Prov. 15:32 NIV

Understanding Discipline

What Is Discipline?

To discipline is to teach. Self-control is one of the most important lessons for young children to learn. And it is through effective discipline that this lesson is taught.

A parent disciplines a child to help him improve his behavior or attitude so that he may become a better and happier person. In disciplining, the highest objective is for your child to learn how to govern his own behavior so that he will not have to rely on the discipline of others.

It is sometimes helpful for parents to differentiate between discipline for the purpose of teaching and punishment for the purpose of forcing children into compliance. An effective parent will constantly be disciplining (teaching acceptable behavior) but he will not necessarily punish! Punishment suggests pain, loss or suffering. It is inflicted on a person as a penalty for wrongdoing. The threat of punishment often frightens children into compliance. It has little to do with effectively teaching them how to govern their own actions when the threat of punishment has been removed. Often a parent punishes to satisfy his own anger. And punishment with anger is never effective discipline. Anger causes you to say things that destroy your child's self-confidence. An example is, "Can't you do anything right?" Or anger may cause you to do things that destroy your child's self-respect, such as impulsively hitting him or unreasonably isolating him and telling others that he has been a naughty child.

Actions like these do not teach your child self-control. They teach him (1) to harbor hateful feelings toward you, (2) to plan ways of revenge, (3) that he is not a very good person, and (4) that if you are bigger it is alright to say or do hurtful things to others.

We have strong Biblical counsel against making our children angry. (Ephesians 6:4) And too often, punishment evokes negative feelings in a child, such as hatred. humiliation and disrespect. This is especially true if the child feels the punishment is unjust.

Effective discipline, on the other hand, *teaches* your child how to bring his actions under control. That's what this chapter is all about!

Prerequisites for Effective Discipline

Establish rapport. The first ingredient for effective discipline is the rapport you have established with your child. This rapport is developed by showing your child that he is accepted, understood, and loved and that you enjoy being close to him. When a child experiences this warmth, he naturally wants to please you by doing what is asked of him. The child who is unsure about his relationship to you and your feelings toward him is the child who is often testing the limits in order to see how you will respond. (See Chapter 3, under "Jealousy.")

All children will at times, without thinking or sometimes intentionally, do things which require discipline. For the most part, disciplining can be handled in such a way that the rapport between you and your child is never broken; for example, holding him close until he gains control of his behavior or talking to him about what has happened.

When on occasion, the conflict between you and your child reaches such a point that your rapport is broken, it is very important for you to have a positive, warm encounter with him as soon as possible. One example would be to hold your child and read to him; or look for something you can praise him for, such as tying his shoes, choosing a nice shirt or dress to wear or making his bed. This will help your child to realize that it is not him that you disapprove of, but his occasional out-of-bounds behavior.

Establish yourself as an authority. Most of us think of an "authority" as someone who holds the reins quite tight and who strictly enforces the rules. But another definition of "authority" is "a specialist." For example, a scholar who is known as an authority has made a certain field of study his specialty. Others look to this type of authority with feelings of respect and confidence. This is the kind of authority parents need to be. We must become specialists in understanding children so we will treat them in a way that will elicit respect. The specialist doesn't establish himself as an authority by saying, "Now, these are the rules. You'll have to live by them. What I say is right." No. He is an open individual who has become an authority as a result of his mastery of his field. When you become that kind of specialist, your children will respect you as an authority.

For discipline to be effective, children must learn that you mean what you say and will follow through on it. Children need to learn to trust what you say because you are the parent, even though they may not understand fully the reason for it. When this lesson is learned, your child is spared the confusion of testing and doubting everything you request or say.

When you are teaching your children the lesson of

parental authority you must beware of distraction techniques that children often employ. "How come I have to do it?" "That's not fair." "Why do you always ask me to do it and never Suzie?" "I'm hungry, can't I eat first?"

Your tendency is to respond and before you know it you're bogged down in an argument and the request is forgotten. If the child responds to your request with a comment, you must quickly decide whether or not it is legitimate. Ignore it, if it's merely a technique to distract you and to prolong the necessity of fulfilling your request. Just repeat your request once again. If he comments again, keep ignoring it and firmly repeat your request until your child gets the idea that you mean business.

Teaching your child that you are an authority does not have to be done with harshness and commanding words. Parents who hold themselves in reserve and exercise their authority in a cold, unsympathizing manner don't win the love of their children. Instead, gather your children close, show them you love them, show an interest in their activities and play with them. You'll not only make your children happy, but you will gain their love and win their confidence. When you spend time establishing rapport it's easier for your children to respect your authority.

To begin establishing yourself as an authority try the following:

1. At first require your child to do only things that can be enforced. This begins at a very early age. For example, say pleasantly and clearly, "Wash your hands." If your child does not respond, you can take him over to the sink, turn on the water and help him wash his hands. A child generally enjoys being independent and will not allow this to happen for very long.

Requests that can't be enforced usually have something to do with a child's control of his body: sleep-

ing, eating, crying or eliminating. In these areas he ultimately has control. Telling your child to "stop crying" or
"go to sleep" is really asking him to do things that you
can't enforce; something a perceptive and strong-willed
child will soon discover.

2. Make the request only once before enforcing it. If
you are sure your child has heard and understood what
is expected, then the request should not be repeated.
Repeating only trains you to nag and your child not to
listen.

3. Don't make too many demands upon your child.
It is best to start out with one request, and when he
learns to respond to this, add other requests that can be
enforced. For example, after your child learns to wash
his hands when he is asked to, then add other requests
such as "Come to the table," "Use your napkin," etc.
All of these requests can be enforced.

4. After your child has learned to respond to the requests that can be enforced, you can begin asking him
to do things that are not as easy to enforce. For example, "Eat your dinner," "Close your eyes and try to
sleep," etc.

To be a successful disciplinarian, you must limit the
requests you make of your child. The requests you do
make need to be stated in a firm, matter-of-fact, "I-mean-
it" voice. If you then follow through on those requests
to make sure your child complies, it is not long before
he gains respect for your authority.

As in all other parent-child relationships, it is most important that disciplining be done in an atmosphere of
warmth and love.

Be consistent. For your child to feel secure he must
be assured that there is some order to his world; he must
have some idea about how each adult who cares for him
will react in certain situations. Consistency is the
keyword, and there are many aspects of consistency that

are important.

1. Be consistent in following through on the requests you make of your children. If one time you say, "It's time to come in now," and make your children stop everything they are doing in order to go inside, while the next time you say, "Come in now," and then let then play outside another fifteen minutes with no explanation, your children will never know quite what to do when you ask them to come in.

Inconsistency in following through on what you request leads to inconsistency in your child's obedience to your requests. For example, Jim knows that the eleventh commandment in his house is, "Thou shalt make your bed," but half the time his mother never checks and his bed goes unmade without comment. So when Jim wakes up in the morning, he unconsciously reasons, "Well, should I make my bed or not? Fifty-fifty Mom won't even notice, so I guess I'll take my chance today and leave it unmade!" Parental inconsistency leads to child inconsistency!

2. Be consistent in the methods of discipline used for a certain misbehavior. Children feel secure when they know how you will react to a given situation. For example, it is good for children to know that if they are disturbing worship they will be asked to leave. If during one disturbance you make your child leave but the next time you ignore his behavior, your children never know what to expect. They will more often than not, take their chances that you will ignore the disturbance. Consistency in this respect will help your child learn the consequences of his behavior. Thus, he can make a rational choice about how he wants to behave.

When children misbehave because adults are not consistent in dealing with them, the adults are the ones at fault.

3. Parents should work together to maintain limits and to handle behavior problems consistently. The

parents — and any other adults living in your home or caring for your children — must keep from revealing any differences in their methods of discipline. As far as the children are concerned, the adults should support one another. In the same respect, children are easily confused when there are a number of caregivers, each with his own idea about what is safe and acceptable behavior. At one time it may be alright to stand on a swing, while at another time it is forbidden.   It is also difficult for a child to learn a new way of behaving when each adult is trying to teach behavior in a different way. For example, one person may be praising the child when he is acting in an acceptable way, and trying to ignore the child's negative behavior when it occurs. If this information is not communicated to the other parent or adults, they may make a big thing about the child's misbehavior. This will have just the opposite effect of what the first parent is working for and trying to teach the child. He learns from the first one that he gets attention when he is behaving, and he learns from the second person that he gets attention when he is misbehaving.

4. As much as possible there should be consistency between the home and school in terms of the expectations parents and teachers have for a child. Where these differ, it should be explained to your child, so that he will have a reason for these inconsistencies and be able to adjust to the differences. For example, your child may need to learn that it is acceptable to finger-paint on the table at school but not at home. At home he can play outside by himself but not at school.

Avoid conflict. In a conflict somebody always loses and too often it's the parent! Here's what happens: Parents try to win by relying on their authority and power, for example, by yelling at the child or even ultimately spanking him. When this happens, even though the child may finally comply because there is really no other choice, the parent is the "winner" only because of force. The child learns nothing about self-control.

The answer is to try in all possible ways to keep on your child's side while at the same time enforcing a requirement. For example, the comment, "You can't have the ball," will lead to a conflict more often than the comment, "I know you want the ball, but John has it now." The first comment does not take your child's feelings into consideration and immediately places you on the opposite side. The second comment, however, places you on the same side as your child by expressing your understanding of his feelings, but at the same time explaining the reality of the situation.

In order to prevent as much conflict as possible, you should remember the following:

1. Do not lose control of yourself. If you are in danger of losing control, it is best to walk away from the situation for a few minutes and pray for guidance. This "time out" will not only give you an opportunity to reflect upon the situation and come to some decision about how it should be handled, but it will also give your child an opportunity to cool down. Very often when this is done, your child feels sorry for his behavior, changes it, and very little else has to be said about the situation.

2. Intervene only when it is actually necessary. In order to determine when you should intervene, it is helpful to divide your child's behavior into three categories: (1) things you like, (2) things you don't like but can tolerate, and (3) things you don't like and cannot tolerate. The way to deal with the first category is to praise these behaviors. The way to deal with the third category is to discipline using a method such as a time-out period, logical consequences or another technique discussed later in this chapter.

Many parents find that most undesirable behavior can fit into the second category. Examples might sometimes include whining, dawdling, bedwetting, occasional un-tidiness if a child is usually neat, putting shoes on the wrong foot, etc. Many of these behaviors are either at-tention-getting devices, age related and will automatical-ly be outgrown, or can be dealt with in a creative way without confronting the issue directly. The more of your child's undesirable behaviors you can put into this sec-ond category, the less conflicts you and your child are likely to have.

Learning by experience and mistakes is often a very effective method of learning. Giving your child a chance to work problems out himself, will often keep you from having to become involved with him in a disciplinary way, thus avoiding a potential conflict.

3. Be flexible in the methods of discipline you use. Each child is different and will respond differently to discipline. For example, one child will stop immediate-ly when you ask him to, while another will stop only when you walk over and stand next to him. Separation may work very well for one child, but it may frighten another child. You must know your children enough to predict which methods of discipline will be effective and which will only lead to more conflict.

4. Win your child's confidence. When your child can understand that you are not against him and are really teaching him or disciplining him so he will be happier and other children will like him better, he will be more likely to respond positively.

5. Try humor to relieve a tension-filled situation. If both you and your child can laugh about the situation, it often helps to clear the air so you both can talk about the problem without becoming upset.

6. Do the opposite of what your child expects. If you do not know how to handle a situation, it sometimes helps to figure out what you think your child expects you to do and then surprise him by doing the opposite.

For example, John is angry at you and marks on the wall with crayons. He expects you to tell him he must clean it up. This requirement may lead to a royal battle because of the mood he is in. Instead, give him a piece of paper and sit down and color with him. After you're both having fun together, cleaning up can become a game, while at the same time, your child may be ready to talk about what caused his anger in the first place. Because you have defused his anger, he now becomes more accepting of your discipline as you say in a firm voice, "Marking on the wall is unacceptable and the consequence is, you must scrub off the marks."

Plan the home environment. A carefully planned schedule and environment will help children to regulate their own behavior, while a disorganized, irregular program will only lead to many discipline problems. It is important that the home be organized in such a way that one activity will not interfere with another. For example, when the blocks are placed next to a doorway where there is a lot of traffic, the chance is greater that the buildings will get knocked down accidently. This arrangement will only lead to problems. If you have a number of children in your family, or care for other children, the quiet areas need to be removed from areas of more boisterous play. A table should be placed next to shelves with puzzles and small toys. Art materials need to be placed close to a sink and on an easy-to-clean surface to facilitate cleaning up. A well-planned playroom environment includes blocks sorted on a shelf and toys placed where your children can get them and put them back, rather than in a large disorganized toy box. When the room is arranged in this way, your children are able to learn how to find what they want to play with and put it back. This not only helps them become independent, but it also helps them take an active part in their self-government.

A regular routine is a part of any well-planned program. It is one of the most helpful techniques for influencing children to establish self-control in situations in which they do not have any choice. It helps children to feel secure and to anticipate activities or changes in activities that are routinely planned. For example, if naptime comes after the routine of storytime, washing hands, eating and a bathroom stop, your child will be better able to accept the idea that he must rest than if he never knows when he will be asked to take a nap.

Define limits. Limits should be clearly defined and maintained. The child who knows what behavior is not accepted will feel more secure and will be better able to control himself. Many parents are inconsistent in the maintenance of limits because they have made so many limitations on their children that neither they nor the children can remember them all. The fewer the limits the better. Try these three rules: (1) You may not hurt yourself, (2) you may not hurt others, and (3) you may not hurt things. Every limitation can be based upon these easy-to-remember rules. If your child starts to run out into the street you can say, "You may not run into the street, because you must not hurt yourself. You may play in the yard." If your child hits another child, "You may not hit, because you must not hurt others. You may use your hands to help." If your child starts to scribble on the table, "You may not scribble on the table, because you must not hurt things. You may scribble on this paper."

These rules form the basis of your child's self-discipline. When he has a question about doing something, he can ask himself, "Will it hurt me, others or things?" If the answer is "no" it's probably alright to do it.

General Guidelines

Omit the moralizing. Parents must always remember to criticize the act but never the person. Sermons on what you think caused your child to misbehave or long periods of talking about it are seldom helpful. He needs to be told clearly and simply that what he did was not allowed, yet at the same time you need to show that you like him. Do not say things like, "Now, was that a nice thing to do?" or "Nice people don't do that." This implies that he is a bad person, destroying his feeling of self-worth. If your child knows he has done wrong, don't keep bringing the matter up or criticizing him for his behavior. Your child should never feel that *he* is being criticized. It is only his *behavior* that you disapproved of. It is a good policy never to blame a child for his mistakes or to criticize him in front of others.

Consider the motives. Most children, before the age of six or seven, feel that if they do something wrong or break or destroy something, they deserve an amount of punishment related to the amount of destruction, regardless of what their motive for the act may have been. For example, if a preschool child is told the following story: "One boy was mad at his mother and threw down a cup and broke it, while another boy was trying to help his mother and dropped a whole armload of dishes and broke them," and then asked, "Which boy deserves the greater punishment?" the child will typically say, "the boy who broke the most," and disregard the motives behind the act. This response is characteristic of a young child's thinking. Parents may contribute to this erroneous thinking by over-reacting to the offense; sometimes punishing severely for something that was an accident.

Discipline should be given according to the motives for the act rather than the consequences. For example, if a child breaks something accidentally, his feelings of remorse will often be enough of a consequence to remind him to be careful in the future. However, if he intentionally breaks something because he is angry, then action must be taken to teach the child that this is unacceptable. When children are punished for something which was a mistake, it often makes them angry at their parent for their lack of understanding. This anger, caused by what they perceive as unfair treatment, may lead to further aggression and destructiveness.

Be positive. Make positive requests of your children. Instead of saying, "Don't stand on the table," say, "Stand on the floor." This lets your child know what behavior is acceptable and gives him a directive to follow. "Don't stand on the table," doesn't emphasize to a child an acceptable alternative.

Threats such as, "If you hit her again —" are ineffective. Most children hear only the "hit her again," which is usually what they do! Be aware that parents cause many behavior problems in their children by over-reacting to their negative behavior. Children soon learn what causes parents to explode. When your child is angry and wants to get back at you, he does the forbidden.

Avoid the idiot "no." An idiot "no" is simply a reflex action or the consequence of a foul mood. Say to yourself, "Is this 'no' necessary or is it an idiot 'no?'" Your child's die of "no's" must not be too rich or the "no" will become commonplace and ineffective. Parents often get into difficulty by immediately saying, "No" to a child's request rather than thinking about the request and seeing if there is a possibility of fulfilling it. For example, a child says, "Can I go outside?" The parent responds, "No."

Child: "Why not?"

Parent: "Because all of the other children are inside, and I need to be inside."

Child: "Why do you need to be with me?"

Parent: "To protect you."

Child: "From what?"

Parent: "I said, 'No.'"

Child: "Mrs. Jones from next door is outside. Why can't she watch me?"

Parent: "I said, 'No.'"

Child: "Why not?"

And before the parent realizes it, she sees that she didn't have a good reason for saying, "No" in the first place and changes her mind and says, "Yes." This kind of dialogue teaches your child two things: (1) Your "no" is not very meaningful; and (2) if I nag long enough, I can change my parent's mind. This incident should not be interpreted to mean that once you say something you should never change your mind, even though you later realize that you have made a mistake. You should acknowledge that you didn't have a good reason for saying, "No" in the first place and now realize that it really wouldn't hurt for your child to go outside. But it is always better to restrict the "no's" to the essentials.

Save face. Don't put either yourself or your child in an impossible situation. Leave him and yourself a gracious way out. Do not threaten him with something you can't or aren't willing to carry out. For example, "If you do it again, I'm going to call your father" knowing that he's out of the office for the day.

Do not extract promises from your child which he isn't likely to remember. For example, "Promise me that you will never hit anybody again."

Do not expect your child to do things he is not likely to do except by your taking him by the scruff of the neck. For example, "Eat every one of those peas."

Do not allow your child to make a choice when you really didn't mean for him to have that choice. Avoid saying, "What would you like to play with?" This gives him the opportunity to choose something you don't have available. Instead, say, "Do you want to play with the blocks, the puzzles or the paint?"

Anticipate difficulties. If you can anticipate difficulties and forewarn your child, it will help him to gain control of himself before he loses it. For example, if he is playing with another child's toy and you know the other child will be furious, help your child find something else of interest. Many of the things children do that parents feel must be corrected would never happen if only parents were more observant and would help him rechannel his behavior before misbehaviors occur. Here are effective techniques to use when you anticipate difficulties.

1. *Touch control.* Many discipline problems occur because the parent is not observant enough to notice that tensions are rising or conflicts are starting. Before things explode, sometimes a gentle pat, an embrace or simply placing a hand on your child's shoulder will serve as a reminder that you are near and will help him when he needs help. If your touch is properly timed, it may prevent your child from becoming unmanageably aggressive. Touch control is effective only if you are aware of the gathering storm clouds. It should always be gentle, warm and reassuring.

2. *"Hypodermic" affection.* A friendly injection of affection may give your child a quick boost over a difficult situation. This can be done verbally by saying, "I love you," or "You look lovely." It can be done nonverbally with a smile, a wink or a spontaneous hug. Children need adult reassurance that they are loved and accepted. This adult support helps them to establish their own self-control.

3. *Diversion.* When your child becomes frustrated and can't seem to handle the situation even with adult help, diversion to an activity he can find success and an interest in may help him to refocus. This is especially important when children are too young to reason with. When diverting a child's attention to another activity, it is important to find an activity as closely related to the desired activity as possible. For example, if your child

starts to throw blocks, a desirable diversion activity might be to throw bean bags into a basket, or rings onto a peg, rather than sitting down and cutting paper.

4. *Point out reality.* Parents are often surprised at how soon it is possible to reason with a child. Even tiny two-year-olds can understand simple reasoning when they want to. Many children become frustrated because they want to do something, but there isn't enough time or space, or the right tools are not available. They become angry and aggressive because they do not understand these limitations. Parents should take the extra time required to explain the reality of the situation and point out what can be done within these limitations. For example, "I don't have the ingredients to make ice cream, but I do have a package of pudding we can make." When you are reasoning with a child, it is important that the explanation be short and simple.

A direct appeal for the child's cooperation is often effective with older children. They like to please and be helpful and will usually listen to this direct pointing out of reality. For example, "You need to pay attention to the story because the others want to hear it."

5. *Use incentives* and rewards. Promises and rewards should not be used to bribe a child. For example, "If you are good today, I'll give you a surprise." However, it may, at times, be appropriate to use promises and rewards as an incentive for desirable behavior. For example, "If you pick up the puzzles, we may have time for a story before lunch." It is also acceptable to use promises and rewards as an alternative to behavior or activities which are not allowed. You might say, "We can't go to the zoo today but we can go skating." Before promising anything, you must be sure you are able to fulfill that promise. If you're uncertain about whether you can fulfill a promise, then you should be careful to make it clear to your child that there are certain conditions. For

example, "We can go to the park tomorrow, if it doesn't rain."

It is better to use rewards as an incentive for good behavior than to be reprimanding a child constantly for unacceptable behavior.

Techniques of discipline

Natural and imposed logical consequences. Letting children experience the natural consequence of their behavior is one of the most effective ways for them to learn more appropriate ways of behaving. It is important that you do not step into a conflict or situation too quickly and solve every problem for your child. Some things are learned much more quickly and effectively if we allow children to "suffer" the natural consequences of their mistakes. No reprimand or moralizing is necessary. The child knows he made a mistake, reaps the consequences, and will be wiser the next time. Almost every infraction of a limitation has a natural consequence. If a child doesn't put his things in his closet, he can't find them when he wants them; if he doesn't come when you announce dinner, he misses it; if he doesn't put his dirty clothes in the hamper, they aren't washed, etc.

Since for some behavior the natural consequence is more serious, it's a good idea for you to point out the consequences in order to give your child a reason for discontinuing that behavior. For example, "Johnny is bigger than you are. If you hit him, he will probably hit you back, and it will hurt. How else could you handle this problem?"

If there is no natural consequence to a child's inappropriate behavior, or if the natural consequence is physically or psychologically harmful, then parents must impose a logical consequence. "Logical" is the key word. In order for consequences to be most effective they should "fit the crime." For example, if a child breaks a window, the parent-imposed logical consequence might be that the child must help pay for it. If milk is spilled, the child needs to clean it up. If the children are being mean to each other, they need to be separated. Even young children can see the reason for these consequences, and seldom feel that they have been dealt with unfairly.

Isolation or a time-out period is often used as a logical consequence of a child's misbehavior. If he cannot cooperate and be kind to others, then he loses his right to be with them. It is not necessary for you to make the isolation of your child an unpleasant experience in order for the lesson to be learned. Usually just being deprived of the opportunity to play with his friends is enough. When you isolate your child, it is a good idea to give him something to do. When a child is left sitting in a corner with nothing to do, it gives him an opportunity to think up all kinds of evil thoughts about the person who is imposing this "discipline." It would be much better to give your child something quiet to entertain him or a book to read until he feels that he is ready to get along without causing trouble.

Withholding privileges from a child is often considered a logical consequence of a child's misbehavior. In some situations this is justified. For example, if your child does not eat his lunch, he gets no dessert. But in other situations this is not acceptable. For example, it is not logical for you to hold the threat of having a privilege taken away unless your child conforms, when the privilege has no relationship to his present behavior. For example, you should not say to your child, "Stop hitting right now, or I will not allow you to have any dessert." In this situation it would be better to say, "Stop hitting right now, or you will not be able to play with Bill for a while since you can't get along together."

Children may feel bad when they make mistakes and

have to suffer the consequences. Encourage them to accept the consequences positively by teaching them that every mistake, every fault, every difficulty conquered becomes a steppingstone to better things.

Praise the positive — ignore the negative. This disciplinary technique is an effective method of behavior modification. All children want attention and praise and will pattern their behavior in the ways that will bring them as much attention and praise as possible. The key is for you to be observant and spend time with your children when they are happy and behaving in appropriate ways. The child who usually catches the parent's attention is the misbehaving child. Unfortunately many parents end up spending most of their time with children when they are misbehaving. This tends to reinforce negative behavior.

Not every infringement has to be dealt with immediately. The following situations might be best handled by ignoring the behavior:

1. When your child is frustrated or is wearing his emotions on his sleeve, the slightest comment may bring an explosion. He will probably be deaf to your pleas anyway. Waiting until he cools down will give him the attention he desires at a time when he is acting appropriately. At this same time he is also better able to listen and learn.

2. Leave your child alone during a temper tantrum. Children do not really enjoy throwing them; often they do it only for the effect it has upon the parent and the attention that it usually brings.

3. When your child is deliberately doing something to try to annoy you or get your attention, don't fall into his trap.

4. Ignore behavior you don't like, but can tolerate such as wetting the bed, sucking on a pacifier, or whining. Often your child will outgrow it.

Ignoring your child's misbehavior may be an effective method of behavior modification. But ignoring does not mean being indifferent. Although you may deliberately ignore the behavior at the time, you may later want to talk to your child about his inappropriate actions so there is no misunderstanding in his mind about your expectations.

One way to avoid rewarding negative behavior is to use a "time-out" period. Immediately after the child has misbehaved say, "Time out for . . . ." Usually five minutes alone in his room and away from anyone who will give him attention will be enough to make an impact. It is especially important to control your body language, facial expressions and tone of voice when announcing and enforcing a "time-out." Expressions of disgust, exasperation or annoyance will give your child the message that he succeeded in getting to you. Be firm but matter-of-fact.

Before ignoring your child's negative behavior, it is important that you consider the following questions: (1) Will it be destructive to this child to ignore him? (2) Will it be destructive to property? (3) Will it be destructive to the other children? It may be destructive to your child if he thinks he is getting away with something; and when this goes uncorrected, the tendency for wrongdoing is strengthened. Of course, it would be destructive to your child if there is a chance he might hurt himself. It may be destructive to property if your child is pounding on a table or throwing toys. Finally, it may be destructive to other children if they see a child getting away with disobeying. It may lower their respect for you as an authority.

This method of disciplining — praising the positive, ignoring the negative — is based upon the principle that a problem child acts the way he does, not because he was born that way, but because he has learned (you might say, he was taught) to behave that way through the rewards or reinforcement he was given. These rewards may have been anything from something positive like a piece of candy or hugs and kisses, to a spanking. Yes, a spanking is a reward if a child wants attention, and after misbehaving by, let's say, hitting another child, he finally gets your attention and you end up spanking him. In this case, perhaps the only way of not rewarding the child's hitting would be to ignore his behavior and give all your attention to the child that was hit.

For children, immediate rewards are the most effective. When you tell your child, "Thank you for putting the blocks away," two seconds after he did it, you will be more successful in reinforcing that desirable behavior than if you who wait five minutes before telling your child "thank you." When you are trying to teach your child appropriate behavior, it is also important not to wait until he has accomplished the whole task before praising him. For example, if you want to teach your child to pick up the blocks after he is finished with them, you should start by praising him after he puts the first block away.

Random rewards are most effective in maintaining learned behavior. As your child learns what is expected of him, you can withhold praise until more and more of the task is accomplished. Finally, when he consistently puts away all the blocks, you don't need to reinforce his behavior every time. The reward as a reinforcer then becomes more effective if it is used randomly, sometimes praising and once in a while, not. At this point, not praising is really an expression of confidence that you knew all along he would do the task. It's no longer a milestone for him and only occasional praise and appreciation are necessary or appropriate.

There are two kinds of reinforcers, the social (a smile, a word of praise, a hug) and the nonsocial (points, raisins, stars, etc.). For most children, a social reinforcement is more important than a nonsocial. These are children who have a positive relationship with adults and enjoy pleasing them and having their attention. For a minority of children, it may be necessary to give them something more tangible and something they desire very highly. Something to eat, such as raisins, may be the most effective. When a child must wait until lunchtime to eat these reinforcers, some of their effectiveness will be lost. But in most cases they will still be more meaningful than something abstract like points or stars. The unique aspect of points or stars is that they can be accumulated. When the child has a certain number, they can be traded in for something he wants very much, such as a toy or a trip to the park.

When you apply this method, it is important to work on only one behavior at a time. In order to evaluate the effectiveness of the discipline, you must know how often the undesirable behavior is happening. This can be done by counting how many times it happens in one hour, three hours or one day. Then, after the reinforcement program is started, re-evaluate your child's behavior periodically to see if any progress has been made.

When you decide on a type of discipline to use with a certain child, it is extremely important that you communicate this to all members of the family so the child can be rewarded or ignored consistently.

Spanking. As a general guideline, spanking should be avoided, and slapping, jerking or shaking should be outlawed. The problem of spanking is similar to that of other physical discipline; it is usually done when the tensions of both child and parent are high and the parent is finally driven to administer the punishment in anger.

When a parent is angry there is a danger of losing self-control. When you correct a child in anger you are probably more at fault than your child.

Another danger is that spanking in anger sets a bad

example for your child. When children see someone else hitting, especially when that person gets away with it, they will easily copy that action. The ineffectiveness of physical punishment is revealed in colorful statements by a Christian author, "To shake a child would shake two evil spirits in, while it would shake one out. If a child is wrong, to shake it only makes it worse."[6]

It is also true that physical punishment, if used indiscriminately, may interfere with the development of a child's conscience. Spanking relieves guilt too easily; the child, having paid for his misbehavior, feels free to repeat it.

Some children who feel that they have been ignored and rejected in their homes try to get their parents' attention by being mischievous and naughty. They continue these undesirable actions until their parents, in anger, resort to spanking them. After punishing their children, these parents often feel sorry for what they have done and try to make it up to the child by hugging, kissing and holding him. This is the only way some children have found to get the loving attention they need. A much better way to handle this situation would be to give the child the attention he desires when he is not misbehaving.

Is a spanking ever the best way to teach a child acceptable behavior? A spanking may be an acceptable form of discipline when a young child is rebelling against his parent's authority and all other methods of discipline fail to teach him this most important lesson. This may be the only way you will be able to get through to a particularily strong-willed child. Often, one such correction is all that a child will need, to learn that parents have authority to enforce certain limitations. But you shouldn't spank your child unless you can, with a clear conscience, ask God's blessing upon the correction.

Remember, in most cases there is probably a more effective and Christlike method of teaching your child appropriate behavior than spanking. It may take a little time and creativity, but I would challenge you to put your greatest effort into being a wise and understanding disciplinarian, and you'll enjoy the fruits of your labor for a lifetime.

Example. Parents are examples to their child in everything they do. This example has much to do with their children's formation of character. But it is not enough just to live a Christlike life; you must also point out to your child the principles behind living happily and successfully with others. This pointing out of principle is teaching, and the teaching is discipline.

Remember, there is power in prayer. When all else fails, and you're faced with having to administer strict discipline, such as a spanking, because a rebellious child will not respond to milder training, prayer often works a miracle upon the child's heart and he will feel genuinely sorry and willingly ask forgiveness for what he has done. Sometimes no further discipline is necessary.

It is important that you pray for guidance whenever you discipline your children. Ask for wisdom to choose the most effective type of discipline and to know just how it should be administered in order for your child to experience the best learning. Dealing with children is so complex that it is only through a close relationship with Christ that you will gain the understanding needed to deal with the many daily situations that will mold your child's character. If you take time out to pray before you discipline your children, you'll often have a clearer insight into the problem and, in addition, gain your own composure and self-control.

With all of these admonitions, principles, limitations and cautions it may seem as if no person, no matter how much training and experience he has, could reach the standard of consistently using the best method of discipline with each individual child. That may be so. But just as children learn by their mistakes, so do parents. Wise parents recognize this and, through observing the reactions of their children to the discipline they are administering, change and modify their techniques appropriately.

Understanding Self-Worth

How a child feels about himself, whether he sees himself as someone of high value or worthless, is the single greatest factor in determining his future happiness and well-being. Your child may have beauty and brains, riches and talent, and your family may be well known, but if your child personally dislikes himself and feels inferior to others, these assets will be of little benefit to him.

The goal of parents should be to help each child to develop into a fully functioning, happy, competent individual — someone with a healthy sense of self-worth.

A person who has self-worth has respect for himself, his character and his behavior. He believes in himself and, therefore, has the internal strength and confidence to reach out and try something new. If he fails, he is not overwhelmed with feelings of failure and guilt. He is able to pick himself up and start again.

A person with a sense of self-worth feels not only that he is inherently valuable but that he has a contribution to make which will be valued by others. He also feels that he is loved and that he is esteemed by the significant others in his life. In other words, he feels good about himself; and because he feels good about himself, he is better able to feel the same way about others and treat them accordingly.

A child usually values himself to the extent that he feels valued by others — especially the significant others in his life. Parents, family, teachers and friends become like a mirror through which he sees himself. There are dangers if this is his only source of self-worth.

The first danger is that the child may perceive incorrectly. Others may value him, but his perception is faulty. The messages given to him may be colored by someone else's negative emotions or behavior which the child feels are directed toward him because he's not valued.

The second danger is that others might not know him well, so their estimate of him is faulty. In this case, the child is basing his own sense of self-worth on the feedback he gets from people who don't have enough information about him or whose information about him is incorrect. Either way the child loses!

There are five different components that make up feelings about self.

1. Self-image: how a person feels about his physical appearance and material aspects of life.

2. Self-esteem: how a person feels when a comparison is made with others. This is often determined by how popular a child is.

3. Self-confidence: how a person feels based on interaction with his environment using his skills and abilities.

4. Self-respect: how a person feels about his ability to live up to his own value system.

5. Self-worth: how a person feels about his true value based on God's creation and redemption.

Although each of these affect a child's sense of self,

parents must be careful not to promote self-image, self-esteem and self-confidence as major-value factors. These three things are extremely tenuous. One freak accident can completely change a child's self-image. Rejection by the kids in a popular clique can destroy self-esteem. And flunking a class can damage self-confidence. Instead, encourage your children to put the emphasis on self-respect (being true to yourself) and true self-worth (accepting God's value of your life). The emphasis on self-respect and God's value of worth will provide a cushion for your child against the bumps and bruises of life that can damage his sense of worth.

Self-worth can be effected by successes and failures. It is a myth that good things only happen to good people. A child must be taught that life is difficult and often unfair, but that what happens to you (whether good or bad) has nothing to do with your value. Everyone makes mistakes. The important thing is to take the cards that life deals you and play the best hand you can, not letting your failures make you feel worthless.

A child's sense of self is so precious that parents should take precautions never to wound or destroy it. The same factors that empty a child's love cup also destroy his sense of value: expressing approval only when your child is good; ridiculing your child in an attempt to correct him; threatening; expressing a critical attitude; screaming; expressing disappointment or disgust; giving the silent treatment; being too busy; breaking love routines; or using your child's name negatively. Basically, if you don't feel loved, you won't feel very good about yourself.

A good way to understand the vulnerability of a child's self-worth is to think about one's own experience. Ask yourself questions such as these:

How do you feel about yourself?

Why do you think you feel this way? Did your parents or teachers say anything to give you this impression?

How does it make you feel when you are appreciated?

How does it make you feel when someone speaks to you harshly or critically?

How do you feel when someone notices how well you did your job?

How do you feel when you attempt a hard job and you receive no support or encouragement from people around you?

How do you feel when someone says, "I knew you wouldn't be able to do that."?

How do you feel when someone says, "I knew you could do it."?

Comments such as these can help to build or destroy self-worth.

Selfishness, Pride and Self-Worth

Christians sometimes have difficulty understanding the importance of self-worth because of the seemingly fine line that divides the feeling of self-worth (defined as respect for and belief in oneself) from the feeling of pride (defined as conceit or an over-high opinion of oneself). Christians may recall the Bible texts that warn against an exaggerated sense of self-esteem, such as, "Pride goeth before destruction, and an haughty spirit before a fall." Proverbs 16:18. Or they may think of the text in Proverbs 6:17 where "a proud look" heads the list of things that God hates. Christians are well aware that pride and selfisness are traits to be avoided. (Philippians 2:3)

When parents observe young children, they realize that selfishness is a common behavior. Therefore, too many parents reason that the best way to help children overcome selfishness and to protect them from falling prey to pride is to guard against saying anything, or treating their child in any way, that would build his feelings of self-worth. But this reasoning is faulty.

In fact, in most cases, just the opposite is true. When children are surrounded with persons who love and respect them and are open enough to show them, through word and deed, that they are important individuals, the tendency to act bigger or better than others or to talk about their own importance is decreased. It frees them to appreciate and enjoy the accomplishments of others without feeling diminished by comparison or psychologically threatened.

Christian Principles of Self-Worth

In no other area is there such a vast difference between humanistic and Christian philosophy than there is in the understanding of self-worth. Humanistic philosophy says that you are as valuable as you believe you are. The emphasis is on pulling yourself up by your own bootstraps by focusing on positive traits and believing the best about yourself. Only a person with tremendous fortitude can do this when his world falls apart and his friends turn against him.

The Christian approach offers something above and beyond the humanistic. The following principles should help you to understand more clearly how the feeling of genuine self-worth is attained.

Principle 1: *We are valuable to and through Christ.* Christ not only created us, but He died for us. The effect of this on our self-worth is beautifully stated in these words:

"The price paid for our redemption, the infinite sacrifice of our heavenly Father in giving His Son to die for us, should give us exalted conceptions of what we may become through Christ. As the inspired apostle John beheld the height, the depth, the breadth of the Father's love toward the perishing race, he was filled with adoration and reverence; and, failing to find suitable language in which to express the greatness and tenderness of this love, he called upon the world to behold it. 'Behold, what manner of love the Father hath bestowed upon us, that we should be called the sons of God.' 1 John 3:1. What a value this places upon man!''[7]

What an amazing concept, that we are inherently worthy because of Christ and that we need to do nothing to enhance our own worth but to look up to Christ — the "Sun of Righteousness." (Malachi 4:2.) When we look up to Him, we are led to a genuine feeling of value and self-worth! Looking down to ourselves leads to pride and selfishness.

Principle 2: *Greatness comes by reflecting Christ — the Sun of Righteousness.* By reflecting Christ we become valuable to others, and others will respect us.

Since Christ is the source of all greatness, we become worthwhile and valuable to others by reflecting His character and life of service. As a consequence, others will look with respect and admiration upon the person who is genuinely reflecting Christ.

Problems arise when people try to reflect Christ through their own efforts. Just as the moon and the planets do not shine because of their own power or through any virtue or works of their own, but rather reflect the light of the sun, so can we reflect Christ. All we need to do is to be *willing,* and to place ourselves in the right position (a position of close friendship with Him) so that reflection comes naturally. It is our privilege and honor to reflect Christ, and He has promised us that He will make it possible for us to do it.

Principle 3: *We must evaluate our reflection by looking to the Bible standard.* It is not enough just to assume that our reflection is adequate. We must continually seek God's standard for us through reading His Word and listening to His Spirit speak to our hearts. If we are out of line in any area, we must be willing to admit our wrong and correct it before we will be able to accomplish what God seeks for us to accomplish.

Principle 4: *We have a responsibility to teach others about Christ and His teachings.* Fulfilling this responsibility brings self-worth. God gives each person a work to do, and it is in the accomplishment of this God-given work that feelings of self-worth blossom. We must not aim for self-worth directly. It will naturally come as a result of preparing ourselves for the highest possible level of usefulness and by fulfilling the work that God has given each of us to do.

There is nothing wrong in having high aspirations; wanting to be a Nobel-prize-winning scientist, to be elected to the Senate or to be the best mom or dad in the world! God wants everyone to aim to reach the highest possible standard, but not for self-glory. God wants us to cultivate our talents to their highest capacity so we can do a noble work for Him and bless humanity.

Principle 5: *We must encourage children to reflect Christ — not us.* We have a responsibility to help children develop the self-worth needed to be thinkers — reflecting Christ instead of men. If children are to be masters and not slaves of circumstances and have the courage to stand up to their convictions — they must have good feelings of self-worth.

It takes real courage for a child to take a stand for Christian principles when most of his friends are "following the crowd." Children growing up in today's society must make many moral decisions you may never have faced. Preparation for withstanding peer pressure starts in the earliest years. If your child has a solid sense of self-worth, built upon these five principles I've just discussed, his ability to stand for what he believes in will be greatly enhanced.

Children must not forever reflect their parents and

teachers. They must grow toward independence and slowly move out from the reflection of men into the full reflection of Christ. It is the duty of parents to bend the young twig toward the Sun of Righteousness.

During infancy and early childhood your children live within your shadow and must see Christ and sense their own self-worth through you. But as your children grow, they gradually move out from this shadow until, ideally, they will reflect Christ and look to Him for their feelings of self-worth, instead of to you and other significant people in their lives.

It is through learning to look to Christ and recognizing their worth in Him that youth will be able to withstand the influence of their peers. If they are constantly looking to other fallible human beings in their lives for conformation and as a measure of their value, they are vulnerable to undesirable influences. But when they look directly to Christ, the pattern is perfect.

Our goal should be to help children develop such a strong feeling of their worth through Christ that they have the self-confidence to say, "Even though my peers are doing those things, I'm looking to Christ as my example. I want to reflect Christ."

Developing Self-Worth in Children

Young children's concepts of God are formed as they look to parents and other significant adults in their lives. They form their first understanding about God's love as they experience their parents' love, just as they form their first understanding about how God values them as they experience how their parents value them. We can, through our associations with our children, either build or destroy their feelings of self-worth. What a tremendous responsibility this is!

The following section gives some basic guidelines that parents should follow in building children's self-worth.

1. *Have realistically high expectations for each child.*

If we expect children to misbehave, they more than likely will fulfill our expectations. When children are called names, such as "idiot," or "dummy," they may, after hearing these over a long period of time, begin to feel that they aren't very smart. It's as if our words write a negative script for their lives. Children will do their best to live up to the expectations that we have for them. Therefore, it is extremely important that our expectations be good and honorable. At the same time they must be realistic. If we hold unrealistically high expectations for our children, this only brings them discouragement and frustration. It will have an undesirable effect upon their feelings of self-worth.

2. *Help children to develop abilities and skills.*

When a child feels he is capable of doing many things, he feels good about himself. Encouraging your child to develop his abilities and helping him acquire new skills will give him confidence that he *can* learn and that he is a capable individual. Each new area of expertise he masters will mean a new area where he can receive approval and recognition from those around him.

Look for talents that can be developed. Note interests that will motivate a child to devote the time and energy necessary for advancement. Be alert to unique skills your child can develop in areas where there is little competition. For example, he may have a much better chance being first oboe than he would being first trumpet. Or if his small frame doesn't fit him for football, what about skateboarding, gymnastics, swimming or horseback riding?

Open doors of opportunity. You never know what skill God may need your child to have in order to do a special work for Him.

3. *Recognize each child's achievements.*

When a child improves his talents and is successful in an activity, he deserves recognition. There's a place for praise, for appreciation, for letting him know that you approve, for giving honor. Rightful recognition should not lead to selfishness, pride or vanity. Instead, it should lead the children to more readily appreciate the accomplishments of others.

Recognition should be given in such a way that it will not create rivalry, envy, or jealousy. The achieving child should be encouraged to help his siblings and friends achieve the same success, so that none will be discouraged.

Parents, you should be aware of over-generalized compliments or comparisons that may foster an exaggerated sense of self-esteem. For example:

"You're the best in the whole family."

"Everyone, look at what a nice job Mary did."

"I want all of you to do it just as Bill did."

"You always do it just perfectly."

"I'm glad you are never noisy like the rest."

"You're an angel."

These phrases single out one child and place him above the others. If this happens often, your child may begin to feel that he is better than anyone else. On the other hand, he knows that comments such as, "You're always such a good boy," are not true. He knows he has had thoughts and done things that were not desirable. If you over-generalize your child's goodness, it may generate feelings of guilt within him, and this may even lead him to do something overtly bad to set the record straight.

An over-generalized compliment can have the effect of reducing your child's self-worth rather than enhancing it. Since he realizes that whatever was said is not really true, he feels diminished — that he is not as good as he should be — and concerned that in the future he must achieve an unattainable standard to live up to your compliment. He may even become reticent to do the task again for fear it will not come up to the previously expressed expectations.

Keep your comments of recognition specific to the particular occasion. For example, "Johnny, you did a good job of washing your hands today," instead of, "Johnny, you are such a neat boy;" or say, "Johnny, I think that is an interesting tree you painted," instead of "Johnny, you are such a good painter."

4. *Inspire children to serve others.*

When children are inspired to look beyond themselves and do nice things for others, they are happy with themselves and feel good that they have done something kind.

Feelings very often follow actions. For example, it is common for young children to have selfish feelings. But when they are encouraged to serve others, it takes their minds away from themselves and they experience how others react to their acts of service. The appreciation they receive helps to build their feelings of self-worth. The better they feel about themselves, the less they need to feel selfish about their things, and the feeling of generosity is developed.

5. *Encourage children with a sense of hope.*

Life, for any of us, can be discouraging at times. But, for a young child who does not have many inner resources and who is totally dependent upon parents and teachers, life can be a real trial. Children need to be encouraged constantly — encouraged that they can learn appropriate ways of behaving, encouraged that they can develop skills, encouraged that they are liked by those around them. When a child interacts with adults who encourage him and give him a sense of hope of what he may become through Christ's help, he will develop the inner confidence to begin stepping out in faith — to become, indeed, that kind of individual.

6. *Be patient and willing to forgive and to forget.*

Nothing tears down a child's self-worth quite so quickly as to be constantly reminded of his faults and mistakes.

Don't say to your child, "You broke something again? Last week it was the vase, now it's the window. You are always so careless!" Instead, deal creatively with the immediate problem without reference to past mistakes.

Children usually desire to do what is right — that which brings the approval of others. Yet many times they fail. They need adults who are not only forgiving, but who are also willing to "forget" the wrongdoing, and who will not think any less of them for having misbehaved.

7. *Teach children not to use words of retaliation and self-justification.*

The human tendency when something goes wrong is to pass the blame to others rather than to accept one's own responsibility. When children (or adults) speak hastily to defend themselves, they very often portray the other person's actions and motives as worse than their own. Tearing down others to make oneself look better is a very damaging habit for children to acquire, for it ultimately tears down their own self-respect.

8. *Think before you speak.*

Not only can words be damaging to a child's self-worth, but also the manner in which they are delivered. The tone of voice you use has a strong impact on your child's feelings. Words spoken in a calm, unexcited, purposeful manner will show respect to your child, even if they are words of correction.

Whenever you must discipline your child, it is important that the focus of the correction be on the specific act that was undesirable rather than a general attack upon your child. In addition, it is always important to take your child's feelings into account and protect those sensitive feelings. When you show this type of respect for him, his feelings of self-worth can be increased even in a disciplinary situation.

Here are some words and phrases that can build or destroy self-worth.

Words that destroy self-worth:	**Words that build self-worth:**
Why did you do that?	I'll help you clean it up if you'd like.
Can't you ever do anything right?	Tell me about how you feel.
You're driving me crazy.	What would you like to do today?
Why don't you leave me alone?	I'm busy now, but as soon as I've finished, I'll help you.
You deserved what you got.	Johnny hit you because you hit him. What could you do next time so no one gets hit?
You know better than that.	Remember the rule next time, "You may not hurt things."
If I had it to do over, I wouldn't be a parent.	Sometimes I get tired and frustrated but I love you very much.
You'll be sorry.	Before you do that, think about what might happen.
You talk all the time; can't you ever be quiet?	It is time to be quiet, but I'll listen to your story as soon as naptime is over.
People will call you a bully if you continue acting like this.	People don't like to get pushed around. Next time just talk to them.
Wait until I tell your father.	No, I won't tell your father unless you want me to.
You'll have to sit in a corner if you can't behave.	You may choose to sit and listen to the story or play in your room.

Signs of Low Self-Worth

Low self-worth does not develop suddenly. It's a slow process that occurs when a child perceives that the significant people in his life don't think very much of him. In reality, they may love and care for him very much, but his perception is the important factor. If a child feels that his own parents don't love him or don't think that he is as good as other children, his belief in himself will be seriously damaged. Even if parents shower their child with love and support, there may be periods when he feels that other people don't like him or that his friends are rejecting him. When this occurs, his self-esteem may suffer.

The signs of lack of self-worth are age related. For example, excessive thumb sucking might be considered a sign of low self-worth for a seven or eight-year-old, but could be very normal for a one or two-year-old. These signs are also situation related. For example, a certain behavior may occur when the child is with strangers or when he is very tired. This might indicate that he feels insecure only in certain situations or under certain circumstances.

The behaviors listed below might be considered signs of low self-worth for the preschool and school-age child. If your child exhibits some of these signs, *don't* assume that he has an emotional problem. Consider such behavior an indication that your child could use a little more quality time with you to convince him that he is a worthwhile person. After each characteristic of low self-worth, you will find some suggestions for bolstering your child's ego and helping him realize his true value.

Child is unrealistically fearful:

1. *Is afraid to play games because he might not win.* Play noncompetitive games. Give a prize for playing the

game, not for winning. Teach your child strategies or skills that will help him be successful.

2. *Does not ask questions or is afraid to answer questions.* Make it easy for your child to ask questions. Say, "It looks as if you have a good question for me." Encourage questions when you are alone with him or in a safe family setting. Reward him for asking questions by saying, "That's a good question," or "I can tell you were really thinking." In turn, ask your child questions. At first, make sure your questions have simple or obvious answers. Accept all answers by saying something like, "That's an interesting idea."

3. *When asked to do something, child immediately says, "I don't know how."* Reassure your child that it is okay not to know how. Say, "When I was your age I didn't know how either." Offer to do it and "hire" him as your special assistant. Let him do every small part of the task that he is obviously capable of.

4. *Is afraid to try things for the first time, even when a teacher or parent offers help.* Reassure him that it is acceptable to watch. Let him decide when he will try something new. One way to do this is to ask him, "How long do you think you'll want to watch before trying?" After he indicates the amount of time he needs, tell him to let you know when he's ready so you can help him.

5. *Is afraid to be left in a new situation or with a new person.* Stay with your child until he feels comfortable. Ask him to tell you when it is okay for you to leave. Don't appear anxious to go. If you have allowed a reasonable time, you might warn him, "I will have to leave in one hour,"(or 10 minutes). When the hour is up, go to your child and say "Goodbye," tell him when you will return, and leave. Keep your promise by returning on time.

6. *Does not ask for things he needs.* Make it easy for your child to ask. Never belittle him. Reward requests by saying, "I'm glad you asked," and fulfill the request immediately.

Child exhibits unusual or negative behavior:

1. *Cries, pouts, or exhibits other negative behavior when he doesn't win or get his own way.* Ignore the behavior, but acknowledge his feelings. "It makes you sad when you lose or don't get what you want. I sometimes feel that way." Then give your child something positive to do. "This is what I do when I feel that way.... What are some other things you could do to chase away the sad feelings?"

2. *Carries a blanket or pacifier, or has thumb in mouth wherever he goes.* Give your child an extra amount of attention, but don't let him know that this behavior bothers you. Keep him busy. After three years of age a child can make the decision to give up a blanket or pacifier. Let him buy something he really wants in exchange for it. Let him actually give it away to the store clerk. But be sure it's your child's decision!

3. *Exhibits excessive undesirable behavior, such as biting, kicking, hitting, or spitting.* Use the behavior-modification technique of "ignoring" negative behavior and rewarding positive behavior. (See Chapter 4). Realize that these behaviors are indications of a discouraged, unhappy child. Encourage him. Find the little things he does well and capitalize on those. Stop the negative behavior by saying, "I can't let you hurt someone else," but don't belittle your child with criticism.

4. *Seeks attention by doing something prohibited, by acting silly, or by disturbing others.* Ignore the behavior, but say, "I'll bet you'd like me to play with you. Let's go...." Later, tell your child that he can use a magic word to get your attention. Invent a word so you'll both know what it means and your child won't have to resort to inappropriate behavior to get your attention.

5. *Exhibits such behavior as lying, stealing, or otherwise being deceptive.* This behavior is often a cry for attention. Spend more quality time with your child. Don't be critical. Let him know that you can't be deceived. Say simply, "I know you took the knife. The consequence is that you must return it or pay for it." Don't get in an argument about the truth of a statement. If your child tries to argue that his lie is really true, give him the reason it could not be true and show you understand why he feels the way he does. Say, "I saw what happened, but I can tell you really feel strongly about your point of view. That's exactly how you would like it to be, isn't it? How can I help you feel better about it?"

6. *Deliberately hurts others or himself.* Simply say, "You may not hurt others or yourself." Stop him. Hold him. Comfort him. Talk about the situation. "You were really angry. What happened? What else could you do when that happens again?" Make sure he knows that he is special and you won't allow him to hurt himself.

Child is overly concerned about being liked and accepted:

1. *Constantly gives things to people to buy their attention and friendship.* Discourage the constant giving of gifts. Concentrate on showing your child how much you like him because he exists, not because of his gifts. Compliment him on things he can't change; for example, his blue eyes or black curly hair. Spend time with him when it's not related to the receiving of a gift. Explain to him that the most important gift is friendship because that can't be broken or lost. Encourage your child to invite a friend home to play. Help him to make friends without giving gifts.

2. *Brings things from home to get teacher's and children's attention and approval.* Make it a policy that your children can only take things to school for "show

and tell" sessions. Invite the teacher or special friends to visit your home. Let the teacher know why you think your child is doing this and work together to meet his need for attention and approval.

3. *Often asks parent, "Do you love me?" Asks teacher and children, "Do you like me?"* Read the picture book *The Way Mothers Are,* by Mariam Schlein (Chicago: Albert Whitman Co., 1963, available from Parent Scene), to your child daily for a month and let your behavior give him the same "I love you" message. Help him to develop skills and interests that other people admire.

Child exaggerates or is unrealistic about certain situations:

1. *Complains, "They don't like me," or "They won't play with me."* Don't disagree by saying, "That's not true." Use responsive listening techniques to draw your child out. Say, "You must really feel hurt. Tell me more." Finally, encourage him to think of ways to change this situation.

2. *Brags or boasts by saying such things as, "I'm better than you are."* Shock your child by agreeing. "You are an important person and can do a lot of things better than (person's name). Let's list the things you can do better." (Think of the obvious. If a child is smaller, he can crawl through a smaller hole, etc.) Then talk about how everybody can do something better than somebody. But there is always somebody who can do something better than you.

3. *Is jealous when a child, parent, or teacher shows attention to others.* Spend time with him. Reassure him that he is important and that your love for him will never change. When a child's need for love and attention is met, he will not feel jealous.

4. *Blames others for his own mistakes or finds ex-*

cuses for his behavior. Don't accept his behavior. "Defuse" it by showing your child that you understand how he feels. "It makes you feel terrible when you make a mistake, doesn't it? It's hard for anyone to admit they were wrong. It's okay to make mistakes. That's the way we learn."

Child has difficulty with social relationships:

1. *Is extremely competitive with other children and unhappy if he doesn't "win."* De-emphasize competition. Be sure that both your words and behavior give the message that your child is valuable whether or not he wins.

2. *Does not defend self with words or actions.* Encourage your child to stand up for his rights by saying to him, "You are an important person. Don't allow others to hurt you needlessly." Then give him words to use in future situations — for example, "You may not say those things to me." In a safe environment role play the situation so he can practice the words and the tone of voice to use.

3. *Does not initiate contacts with others.* Show your child how to initiate contacts. For example, show a toy to another child or select a child that looks lonely and walk up and say, "Hi, I'm Jim, do you want to play?"

4. *Is critical and judgmental of others; tattles.* Don't accept tattling and don't reward it. Instead, change the topic of conversation and give your child attention when he is not tattling. Talk to the offender in private, not as a direct result of the tattling.

5. *Calls others names, such as "baby," "dummy," or "shrimp," in order to make himself look better.* Stop this behavior. Make up a story that will show him name calling can hurt a child's feelings. After telling the story, ask, "How would you feel if you were that child? Why

do you think the child called his friend those terrible names? What else could he have done, rather than hurt the child by calling him names?'' Make sure your child understands the concept that we feel better about ourselves when we help others feel better about themselves.

6. *Does not participate in group activities.* Don't force him. Let him know it's okay to be a bystander. Give him something special to do. Invite two or three children over to the house. Help your child feel comfortable with a few friends first.

The Challenge: Be Courageous

The path of parenting is not always rosy. There may be thorns, stones and stumbling blocks in the way. Everything I've said about self-worth for children is true also of parents. Parents, you must understand your own worth in Christ apart from your successes and failures in parenting. Even if you understand the principles of true self-worth, there will be times of discouragement. There will be times when obstacles seem insurmountable, when your goals seem impossible to achieve, and when your children seem hopelessly obnoxious.

Parents sometimes become discouraged when they fail to meet the expectations and standards of what they consider to be a good parent. No matter how hard they try, the ideal always seems beyond reach. Others become discouraged when they realize that they are not making the progress they wish they could with a child. Discouragement can also come when a parent does not receive the support he feels he needs from a spouse or the family in order to do his task adequately.

God does not expect anyone to work alone or to do the whole task of parenting by himself. You should not feel guilty when you have done your best and yet seemingly failed. God promises His help. ''I will save your children.'' (Isaiah 49:25)

The answer is not to look down to self and the problems in the pathway, but to look up — up to the stars. The steadfast stars in their untroubled course are a reminder of God's mighty power. And then look beyond to God, the source of all power.

The scriptures say, "Look up into the heavens! Who created all these stars? As a shepherd leads his sheep, calling each by its pet name, and counts them to see that none are lost or strayed, so God does with stars and planets!" (And if for stars and planets, how much more for his children.)

O parents, ". . . how can you say that the Lord doesn't see your troubles and isn't being fair? Don't you yet understand? Don't you know by now that the everlasting God, the Creator of the farthest parts of the earth, never grows faint or weary? No one can fathom the depths of his understanding. He gives power to the tired and worn out, and strength to the weak."

"Fear not, for I am with you. Do not be dismayed. I am your God. I will strengthen you; I will help you; I will uphold you with my victorious right hand." (Isaiah 40:26-29 and 41:10 *The Living Bible*)

Courage and self-worth cannot be separated. God wants each of us to have courage; courage to seek the truth, accept the truth, live by the truth and speak the truth. Truth must be sought in all areas, including the truth about how God would have us care for His children.

The type of courage it takes to seek, accept, live and speak "truth" can come only when a person has a good, positive feeling of self-worth; for it is only then that he trusts himself enough to risk creative and courageous approaches to living and learning.

The challenge for parents is to make the changes that need to be made. Give up erroneous ideas of child rearing, even though they may be hoary with age, because age doesn't make error truth, nor truth error. Parents have for too long followed customs and habits without understanding why or what is best for children. Parents must learn how to train children in the way they should go without hurting and demeaning them in the process. The lessons of love which Christ taught are to be the standard.

It takes "tons" of genuine self-worth to start again on a better path with our families. But with courage we can make changes.

A Closing Thought

Children sometimes remind me of apples. They come in different colors, sizes and shapes. And as apples differ in taste, so children differ in disposition, some being sweet, some bland and others rather tart. Some may even look a little rotten on the outside — and may have already begun to rot on the inside! But despite all these apparent differences, there is a core similarity.

Take any apple and cut it across the core and there appears in the center a beautiful star. So it is with children — within each core is something beautiful, something worthwhile, something of value to be worked with and developed.

So whenever you feel discouraged in your work with children, cut open an apple and let that star remind you of *Christ* — the special star, the Sun of Righteousness — and His *ideals* by which you must set your course. Be reminded of the *value* He places upon each of your children.

Children are God's little treasures on earth. They may need a little polishing, but the value has been built in, by, and through Christ.

Our goal as parents must be to help children to grow into happy, competent, courageous, Christlike individuals.

How is this possible?

It is possible if we look to Christ, the Sun of Righteousness, as our parent, our teacher, our pattern, our guide, our star, and reflect His image to the children He has given us. Through Christ, and the wisdom that He has promised us, we can have a growing and fruitful understanding of each child.

May I sum up the message of this book in a poem I call *Don't Step on the Pansies.*[9]

DON'T STEP ON THE PANSIES

The Master Gardener once said,
  "Suffer the little pansies to grow in My garden."
    Then He handed me the spade.
      "Take care till I return."

But, God,
  I don't know how.
    I've never had a pansy.
      They are so tiny — so frail.

  Trust me with a rose —
    The thorns
      Will protect it
        From my clumsiness.

  Trust me with a tulip
    Safely buried beneath the sod
      To spring forth in new blossom
        After a season of hardship.

  Trust me with an ivy vine,
    Whose tendrils
      Will cling to others
        For support.

  But God — pansies?
    They have no thorns,
      No bulb, no vine.
        Don't trust me with them.

But the Gardener would not listen.

So I changed my prayer.
 OK, God,
   I'll care for the pansies,
    But tell me how.

And God said,
  "Water them with love;
    Weed them with firmness,
     And let them bask in the sunshine of your soul."

Is that all?
  "There is but one thing more you must remember.
   It is the way you care — the way you touch —
    That will produce the most precious blossoms.

   "So walk gently
    Among My little ones.
     Don't step on
      The pansies."

Remembering the words of the Master Gardener,
 I go forth
   To begin my task,
    Whispering this prayer,

   Oh, God,
    Give me light words,
     Light hands,
      And light feet;

So I won't step on the pansies.

                              — Kay Kuzma

References

Chapter 1

1. White, Burton L., *The First Three Years of Life* (Englewood Cliffs, N.J.: Prentice Hall, Inc., 1975).

Chapter 2

2. Chess, Stella, Alexander Thomas and Herbert G. Birch, *Your Child is a Person* (N.Y.: Parallax Publishing Co., Inc., 1965).

3. Moore, Raymond S. and Dorothy N. Moore, *Better Late Than Early* (N.Y.: Reader's Digest-McGraw Hill, 1976).

4. Smith, Lendon H., *Improving Your Child's Behavior Chemistry* (N.Y.: Pocket Books, 1976).

Chapter 3

5. Bandura, Albert and Richard Walters, *Social Learning and Personality Development* (N.Y.: Holt, Rinehard and Winston, 1963).

Chapter 4

6. White, E.G., *Child Guidance* (Nashville, TN: Southern Publishing Association, 1954).

Chapter 5

7. White, E.G., *Steps to Christ* (Washington, D.C.: Review and Herald Publishing Association, 1892).

8. From: Kuzma, Kay, *Working Mothers* (L.A.: Stratford Press, 1981) pp. 167-173. Used by permission.

9. From: Kuzma, Kay, *Don't Step on the Pansies* (Washington, D.C.: Review and Herald Publishing Association, 1979).

Selected Bibliography

Baruch, Dorothy Walter, Ph.D., *New Ways in Discipline* (New York, NY: McGraw-Hill Book Co., Inc., 1949).
Old, yet new!

Briggs, Dorothy Corkille, *Your Child's Self-Esteem*. (New York, NY: Doubleday and Company, Inc., 1970).
Excellent guidelines for developing self-worth.

Campbell, Ross, *How to Really Love Your Child* (Wheaton, IL: Victor Books, 1977).
How to show love through eye contact, physical contact and focused attention.

Dobson, James, *Dare to Discipline* (Wheaton, IL: Tyndale House Publishers, 1970).
James Dobson gives a good wholesome philosophy explaining the importance of balancing love and discipline.

_____, *Hide or Seek* (Old Tappan, NJ: Fleming H. Revell Company, 1974).
A discussion of inferiority and what we can do to counteract it. Especially good for understanding teen-agers.

_____, *The Strong-willed Child* (Wheaton, IL: Tyndale House, 1978).
Good advice for the difficult child. Read carefully. The method that is suggested can be misapplied.

Dodson, Fitzhugh, *How to Parent* (also, *How to Father* and *How to Discipline with Love*) (Los Angeles, CA: Nash Publishing Corporation, 1972).
General child-rearing information.

Dreikurs, Rudolf, *Children: The Challenge* (N.Y.: Hawthorn Books, 1964).
Of the hundreds of theorists writing about children, no one shows a keener understanding of children and why they behave as they do than Dreikurs.

Ginott, Haim G., *Between Parent and Child* (New York, NY: Avon Books, 1965).
This is a gem. It is easy reading and gives helpful hints on how parents and children can talk together to solve problems.

Gordon, Ira J., *Baby Learning Through Baby Play* (New York, NY: St. Martin's Press, 1970).
Pictorial guide of play activities for the first two years of life.

_____, *Child Learning Through Child Play* (New York, NY: St. Martin's Press, 1972).
A similar book geared to preschoolers.

Gordon, Thomas, *PET: Parent Effectiveness Training* (New York, NY: Peter H. Wyden, Inc., 1970).
Explains a no-lose method — for children who verbalize well.

Kuzma, Kay and Jan Kuzma, *Building Character* (Mt. View, CA: Pacific Press Publishing Association, 1979, Available from Parent Scene).
Practical guide for developing Christian character traits in children.

_____, *Filling Your Love Cup* (Redlands, CA: Parent Scene, Inc. 1982).
How to fill your child's love cup through care, respect, acceptance, forgiveness and trust.

_____, *Teaching Your Own Preschool Children* (NY: Doubleday and Co., 1980, Available from Parent Scene).
A guide for getting more out of the preschool years. Filled with learning activities and creative ideas for teaching your children.

_____, *Living with God's Kids* (Redlands, CA: Parent Scene, Inc. 1983).
Twenty-seven practical chapters on all aspects of Christian parenting.

_____, *Working Mothers* (LA: Stratford Press, 1981, Available from Parent Scene).
How to be a busy parent and still make your family your highest priority.

Lansky, Vicki, *Practical Parenting Tips* (Deephaven, MN: Meadowbrook Press, 1982).
Over 1000 great ideas for the new parent.

Moore, Raymond and Dorothy, *Home Grown Kids* (Waco, TX: Word Books, 1981).
A practice handbook for teaching your children at home, starting from birth.

Painter, Genevieve, *Teach Your Baby* (New York, NY: Simon and Schuster, 1971).
Activities for children during the first three years.

Patterson, Gerald R. and Gullion, Elizabeth M, *Living With Children* (Champaign, IL: Research Press, 1973).
This is a programmed instruction booklet on behavior modification. For problem behavior this is excellent.